WHY IS THE
DEVIL
IN MY
GARDEN?

LOREN COVARRUBIAS

Call from the Mountain Media
4453 Clintonville Road
Waterford, MI 48329

Why is the Devil in My Garden? by Loren Covarrubias
Copyright © 2011 by Loren Covarrubias

Why is the Devil in My Garden?
Published by Call from the Mountain Media
Print Division
4453 Clintonville Road
Waterford, MI 48329

Or contact us at:

info@itsanewday.tv
www.itsanewday.tv

ISBN 978-0-9832084-0-2

Printed in the United States of America   First Edition

DEDICATION

I would like to dedicate this book to my wife Bonnie, whose support and prayer has been a vital part of my ability to walk in the things that God has set before me. Bonnie, you have always been willing to do whatever God has asked of you, including standing behind me in what God has asked me to do. Along with my children and my congregation, you have always confidently assured others that my life is about serving God. Thank you for being such a valuable asset to me!

Acknowledgments

As always, my sister Jeanne Cagle has been my advisor and helper in the writing of this book. We think so much alike that she can tell when my written words are not saying what she knows I am intending to say. While correcting my manuscript, she encourages me with positive remarks about the content—what a good balance!

CONTENTS

Contents

PREFACE

Since the beginning of time the devil has been at work frustrating the plans of God for mankind. God understood that we would be taken in by the devil's craftiness, so he warned us not to be ignorant of his devices. He told us to resist the devil and the devil would flee from us. This idea, unfortunately, is foreign to many and as a result we are the victims and the devil becomes the victor.

The Apostle Paul told the Roman church, "And the God of peace will crush Satan under your feet shortly." This scripture is very telling because it makes an important statement. The devil's days are numbered. God will eventually crush him and he is going to use our feet! This fulfills the prophecy given to Adam and Eve at the time of the transgression in the Garden of Eden. Fear and superstition has clouded our understanding of the devil and it is time for us to address this lack of understanding so that we can fully participate in the plan of God based on the Word of God.

For many the devil is an exaggerated foe. We have given the devil power that he does not possess. We are like Dorothy and her companions in the *Wizard of Oz* movie. The wizard in the movie, like the devil does today, hid behind a façade of power when in fact his greatest strength came through his deception. We must not allow ourselves to be deceived by him.

In this book I hope to show you both how to overcome his opposition in your life and also to recognize how he works. Most importantly we need to see his only real power comes when we give it to him. The real issue beginning in the Garden of Eden presents a question to us. Will we take our place in God or will we fall into the temptation of thinking life is better under our control? When we realize it is about us and God we will understand the devil isn't trying to get us on his side but he wants us to take our own side. It is when we become self centered his power increases and he reigns in our life!

—Loren Covarrubias

Chapter One

THE BEGINNING

As early as the third chapter of the Bible, in the book of Genesis, we see the Bible narrative introducing the devil. This, obviously, makes the devil a major player in the story of God. Yet as we start our study, I want to emphasize the importance of seeing the devil in the light of God. If we fail to see the devil in the light of who God is we will make him into a far different creature than who he really is. Much of what people believe about the devil is based upon subjective experiences and the traditions of men rather than the Word of God. In this new day of visitation it is very important that we allow the light of the Word of God to give us a clear understanding of the plans and purposes of God. With this in mind, we have to understand the devil is a part of God's plan. If we fail to understand he is a part of God's plan we will see him as a counter plan outside the will, purpose, and power of God. If we think that way we do not even know who our God is. God is the Almighty. The Almighty God has an eternal plan for the earth that was established before the foundation of the world. As the Almighty God no purpose of His can be withheld from Him.

> *Then Job answered the LORD and said: "I know that You can do everything, And that no purpose of Yours can be withheld from You. You asked, 'Who is this who hides counsel without knowledge?' Therefore I have uttered what I did not **understand**, **Things too wonderful for me, which I did not know**"* (Job 42:1-3).

Many people, just like Job, live in the world without full understanding. Job was caught in a divine struggle that involved the devil or satan as he is called here. The truth of the narrative of Job's life is that it is really a story about Job's personal growth and development. God was working to bring Job into a fuller understanding of himself and his God. This is the synopsis of the story of your life as well. You must understand the struggle of our existence is about what we know about God and what that knowledge eventually does to change us. Job suffered loss in his story, but his loss was not what he had to resist nor was it satan who caused his loss. Job needed to allow the process of God to work in him to bring him to the place of the double portion God had for his life. The double portion is the portion of the firstborn. The story of the Bible is about the first born of God the Father, Jesus Christ, who not only gained His inheritance from the Father He also has gained an inheritance for us. We are called to be heirs with Him.

> *The Spirit Himself bears witness with our spirit that we are children of God, and if children, then heirs—**heirs of God and joint heirs with Christ**, if indeed we suffer with Him, that we may also be glorified together* (Romans 8:16-17).

God's eternal purpose involves bringing a people to the place of sharing His glory. This people will bring glory to God among the nations and even to the principalities and powers in heavenly places. (Eph 3:9-10) There will be suffering to get to this place. The suffering will involve a struggle against the devil but the devil is not the major source of the struggle. The major source of the struggle involves our response to the circumstances and how that response forms and transforms us to the person God has called us to be.

The story of the children of Israel is the example the Scriptures give to us. When they came to the Promised Land they found out it was everything God told them it would be. However, in their eyes there was a problem. There were giants in the land of promise.

When the children of Israel saw the giants they said; "we are like grasshoppers before them" and refused to go forward and face the struggle to gain the land of promise. The issue from God's perspective was not the giants, but the attitude of the children of Israel. They were enemy oriented rather than God oriented and in that condition they lost out on the promise of God. How did God respond? Did He feel sorry for the people? No! God was angry with His people and ready to destroy them all and raise up a new people for His name's sake. Moses' intervention caused God to spare the children of Israel from immediate judgment and let them die slowly over 40 years in the wilderness. The truth for us to grab hold of is His proclamation afterward:

> *Then the LORD said: "I have pardoned, according to your word; **but truly, as I live, all the earth shall be filled with the glory of the LORD**—because all these men **who have seen My glory** and the signs which I did in Egypt and in the wilderness, and have put Me to the test now these ten times, and have not heeded My voice, they certainly shall not see the land of which I swore to their fathers, nor shall any of those who rejected Me see it"* (Numbers 14:20-23).

The children of Israel focused on the enemy and not the glory of God. God's glory is who He is and how that is manifested in the earth. Everything about their journey had been charted by God. The way He led them was a way that would help them and prepare them for the future.

> *Then it came to pass, when Pharaoh had let the people go, that God did not lead them by way of the land of the Philistines, although that was near; for God said, "Lest perhaps the people change their minds when they see war, and return to Egypt"* (Exodus 13:17).

God did not intend for them to fight immediately, because He knew they couldn't handle it. But God had a day and a time when they should have been ready and at that time God's expectation would be different. I believe this is what we need to understand in the body of Christ today. There are things God says we are now ready for that we were not ready for before. It is a new day and a new time and the people of God must prepare themselves to take on the challenges of this present day. God has a greater expectation of us and we must be ready for the time. Part of the readiness will require a new perspective on the Word of God. Certainly a major part of this is to see ourselves in relationship to God and the enemy we face. Before we face our enemy we must see him in the light of God not from our own human perspective.

As it was with the children of Israel so it is in our day. We must press forward against the obstacles knowing that everything is in God's hands. God has charted our steps and the enemy is not only under God's control he can be under ours. I know this is an uncomfortable concept for many people but we must understand the enemy is a part of God's plan. How could it be otherwise if God is the Almighty God? How could we go forth in confidence against the enemy if we think our enemy is a threat to God? There was an enemy in the Promised Land and there was an enemy, a serpent, in the garden. Was the serpent in the garden against God's will? If you will notice in the story of the fall God not only announced His judgment against man He also announced His judgment upon the serpent. There wasn't a conflict there. God made the announcement and it was stated as fact. It wasn't as if God was threatened or motivated by a fear of the serpent. Of course not! All things are created by God and all things exist by Him. (Col 1:16-17) As with all God's creation His judgment stands and is subject to His word. God has a purpose for the devil and when He is done with him He will get rid of him. The devil knows his time is in God's hand. Why don't we?

> *"Therefore rejoice, O heavens, and you who dwell in them! Woe to the inhabitants of the earth and the sea! For the devil has come down to you, having great wrath, because **he knows that he has a short time**"* (Revelation 12:12).

14

The story of the children of Israel tells us the time is in God's hand. God is motivated by His character and principles and this impacts the times of history. God allows the wicked their time but then He also has His time of displacement and judgment.

> *Now when the sun was going down, a deep sleep fell upon Abram; and behold, horror and great darkness fell upon him. Then He said to Abram: "Know certainly that your descendants will be strangers in a land that is not theirs, and will serve them, and they will afflict them four hundred years. And also **the nation whom they serve I will judge;** afterward they shall come out with great possessions. Now as for you, you shall go to your fathers in peace; you shall be buried at a good old age. But in the fourth generation they shall return here, for the iniquity of the Amorites is not yet complete"* (Genesis 15:12-16).

Darkness fills the void until the light shines. When the light shines darkness has to flee. However, sometimes before the light shines and darkness flees God has a work He must accomplish in the darkness. In our struggle He does a work in us to prepare us for what He has for us. The conflict with the devil is not about him and God; it is about him and us. The reason God allowed the devil to come into the garden as the serpent, is the same reason he is in the world today. When Jesus came to the earth He bound the power of the strongman so we could make a spoil of his goods.

> *Or how can one enter a strong man's house and plunder his goods, **unless he first binds the strong man?** And then he will plunder his house. He who is not with Me is against Me, and **he who does not gather with Me scatters abroad*** (Matthew 12:29).

Notice Jesus did not kick him out of the earth. Jesus broke the power and dominion of the devil that had been given to him by man at the fall. Once Jesus Christ accomplished the breaking of his power He left the rest for us. Just like it was in the garden, God gave us a commission and an enemy to overcome. The devil's power and authority in the earth will be determined by our obedience and willingness to walk in the authority God has given to us. If we are going to overcome him we must not be motivated by our fear or by our traditional thinking that is based on human understanding rather than on the Word of God.

Where does most of our understanding of the devil come from? Much, of course, is indeed the fear within us. It is also based on our need to explain things and understand the mysteries of God from our logical process rather than just faithfully accepting the power of the Word. Many early religions were based on a dualistic understanding of good and evil. In a dualistic understanding evil and good both exist and are in conflict with one another. Often time deities were behind these forces. In the thinking of the early Christian who converted from paganism the devil must be the one who takes the place of the evil deity since we only believe in one God. Unfortunately, the end of this thinking often lends itself to the idea that the devil is a god in conflict with the Eternal God. There is no scriptural foundation for such thinking. Many times our reasoning here is that no creature could have been created by a good God to propagate evil in the world. In our thinking there would be no justice in that idea. So we create stories about evil to take the concept outside of God's realm. Although this soothes our conscience about God, it doesn't give God the honor due His name. Could God actually come under threat from any in His creation? Could angels, who have more spiritual insight of heavenly things, really believe they could rebel against God? Demons have more sense to fear God than we have.

> *You believe that there is one God. You do well. Even the* **demons believe—and tremble!** (James 2:19)

The temptation to understand good and evil was the source of the fall in the beginning and is the source of much falling today. When God placed mankind in the garden they were instructed they could enjoy all the trees of the garden except the Tree of Knowledge of Good and Evil. If they ate of this tree they would surely die. The choice God gave to man in the beginning was pursuing peace and security through simple trust in God or trying to gain these attributes through knowledge and personal understanding. The walk of faith God has called us to requires us to live above the human condition and live in the heavenly realm with Him. This is the realm or Kingdom of God. Our human motivations are based upon self-confidence and self-control, which in the end brings us into the realm of the enemy. We should have the faith to operate with the level of knowledge God gives to us and leave the mysteries to God. If we have faith to leave the unknown in God's hands we will also have the faith to defeat the enemy and take the Promised Land!

It is interesting the Tree of Knowledge was the knowledge of good and evil. Many of the misconceptions we have of the devil are based upon our need to explain the realm of evil, which is the realm of the devil. The story of the devil as a fallen angel comes from prevalent stories in the time of the early church. Since human reasoning requires the devil to be evil by choice, the story of a fallen angel fits well into our theories to fully explain our dilemma with the devil being something outside our understanding based on our human experience. The devil is not human so why do we try to fit him into our human realm. Don't live in the world of human understanding alone. This much we must understand about God as the Almighty. Whether by direct action or permission, all things in the end must be His choice to allow. The prophets of old were not at all conflicted by the concept that God was God of everything.

> *That they may know from the rising of the sun to its setting That there is none besides Me. I am the LORD, and there is no other; I form the light and create darkness, I make peace and create calamity; I, the LORD, do all these things* (Isaiah 45:6-7).

If we are to truly have biblical Christianity it must include the revelation of God from the beginning. All our theology must be rooted in the Old Testament with a change of perspective in the New Testament yet still built on the foundation of the Old. In the Old Testament it is very clear that evil was in the hand of God to use for His purpose.

Remember the story of Saul in the Scriptures? Saul was a man chosen of God yet in time he decided he was smarter than God. God had sent him on a mission with very specific instructions. Saul was to be the hand of God's judgment against the Amalekites. Saul was to fight against them and destroy all the people and all they possessed. Saul gathered the people and he won the war. Victory is assured when we walk in obedience to the Word of God. Saul in his human wisdom decided he would keep the king alive and also the best of the sheep, oxen, and lambs. When Saul came back to give his report to the prophet, Samuel, he received the recompense for his disobedience. Samuel killed the King of the Amalekites and announced to Saul the kingdom would be taken from him because he refused to obey God. Not only did he lose his place, the anointing for service left him. After he lost the anointing something came to take its place.

> *But the Spirit of the LORD departed from Saul, and a distressing spirit from the LORD troubled him. And Saul's servants said to him, "Surely, a distressing spirit from God is troubling you"* (1 Samuel 16:14-15).

The literal translation is an evil spirit came to bring fear. The principle is consistent throughout the Scriptures. The door to evil is opened by disobedience. Darkness comes to fill the void when the light quits shining. Saul became a tormented man.

Another example of Scripture in the Old Testament is recorded in 1 Kings 22. King Ahab, who was the evil king of Israel, sought the help of the godly king of Judah to help him fight a war against Syria. Ahab sought the help of the prophets to give him an encouraging word in his endeavors. The godly king, Jehoshaphat, was leery of the prophets of Israel whom he knew to be out of touch with the true God. He suggested they consult the prophet, Micaiah. Ahab did not want to hear from him because he said Micaiah always gave him bad words. Ahab didn't want to hear the truth. Like so many people he was simply looking for affirmation for his own choices. This is a good lesson for us to learn about prophetic ministry. Micaiah not only spoke the truth to the kings but as a seer he shared an important vision he saw in the heavenly realm.

> *"And the LORD said, '**Who will persuade Ahab to go up, that he may fall at Ramoth Gilead?**' So one spoke in this manner, and another spoke in that manner. Then a spirit came forward and stood before the LORD, and said, '**I will persuade him.**' The LORD said to him, '**In what way?**' So he said, '**I will go out and be a lying spirit in the mouth of all his prophets.**' And the LORD said, '**You shall persuade him, and also prevail. Go out and do so.**' Therefore look! The LORD has put a lying spirit in the mouth of all these prophets of yours, and the LORD has declared disaster **against you**"* (1 Kings 22:20-23).

Again, we see the Almighty in the throne of heaven using all things for the purpose of His will. If we choose to walk in presumption the Lord will even help us out. This shows us an important reason why we should walk humbly before God and recognize how dangerous it is to live outside His will. With the Scriptures and the Holy Spirit as our guide, let's press forward into the realm of the Kingdom of God and then help extend that Kingdom to the nations of the earth! This will only be possible if we see our enemies through the divine perspective.

Chapter Two

THE GARDEN

The first encounter with the devil is in the Garden of Eden recorded in Genesis 3. After God had created mankind He placed them in the Garden of Eden to cultivate and guard it. The mandate for mankind was to be fruitful, multiply, and fill up the earth. After giving the mandate for mankind, God placed Adam in the Garden of Eden. This represents individual stewardship. God has a plan for the church and God has a plan for you. I often hear people say that we need to get together to fulfill God's plan. I submit that dominion comes when each person fully commits themselves to the purpose God has for them and then after their commitment is made sees themselves as contributing to the whole. The reason this is so important is to keep each individual focused on the area of their own responsibility. Adam was given a mandate or call but also a warning. You can enjoy all the blessings of the garden but of the Tree of Knowledge of Good and Evil in the midst of the garden you must not eat of it or you will die.

One day the woman was standing next to the tree God had forbidden them to partake of. The first lesson we learn from this is: don't be standing in a position that affords you the opportunity to sin when you don't want to sin. The Bible says the serpent was more cunning than all the beasts of the field the Lord had made. This statement leads us in the wrong direction if we do not take it in the context of the whole knowledge of God about the serpent. Being compared to the other beasts of the field ("he was more subtle than any beast of the field") does not necessarily mean he was classed with them. It is very important here that we understand this is not literally a snake; but the analogy of the snake is used to tell a deeper story. Interestingly enough, not even the story of the creation of man and woman should be seen only in the light of the visible and literal story. When speaking of the marriage union in Ephesians chapter 5 the Apostle Paul says; "this is a profound mystery but I am talking about Christ and the church." This story of the garden is the story of the church, who is the bride of Christ. This bride will produce the seed, which will one day triumph over the serpent. It is important to see the continuity of the plans and purposes of God from the beginning. I want to take you to the book of the Revelation, the last book of the Bible, to see a greater understanding of the serpent by taking a peek at the end of the story.

> *And war broke out in heaven: Michael and his angels fought with the dragon; and the dragon and his angels fought, but they did not prevail, nor was a place found for them in heaven any longer. So **the great dragon was cast out, that serpent of old, called the Devil and Satan,** who deceives the whole world; he was cast to the earth, and his angels were cast out with him* (Revelation 12:7-9).

This Scripture tells us the serpent of old, now seen as a dragon, was also called the devil or satan. The terms dragon and serpent both give insight into the character and work of the devil. The analogy of the serpent is used in his introduction to show the devil as a slithering and secretive creature who comes to an individual to influence them to disobey the commandment of God. The dragon represents this same serpent taking on a bigger role by using the systems of men to influence us to disobey God through the society and world we live in. This is the subject I will deal with towards the end of this book. Let's first explore the concept of the devil as the serpent. Notice if you would the woman is not surprised the serpent is talking. Talking to people is hardly a normal pastime for real snakes and certainly a behavior we would be very surprised by. This unique creature has communication skills and also has the ability to be cunning or crafty. The woman is fooled by the serpent so the narrative is not speaking of a literal snake that would certainly not fit in a category with those who can reason or communicate. This is the devil or satan pure and simple and he has access to the garden with good reason. God has given mankind a choice and there is no real choice if there is not an advocate for the other side. The word devil means accuser, the word satan means adversary. God has allowed the serpent to come and accuse Him falsely and to be an adversary against man for the purpose to which God has called him.

This obviously confirms the fact God does not feel threatened by the devil or his deeds. The devil is not God's adversary but ours. He seeks to hinder us from serving God and trusting in Him. Will we believe his lies or will we learn to trust in God? We need to dispel some of the myths concerning who the devil is so we can fully understand his methods and purpose. We also need to see how he is used for the purpose of God. If you will follow me on this journey through the Scriptures you will see the serpent is not a good angel gone bad, but he is a creature operating according to his nature. His nature has not changed since his creation. What he was in the garden is what he was from his beginning.

> *You are of your father the devil, and the desires of your father you want to do. He was a **murderer from the beginning**, and does not stand in the truth, because there is no truth in him. **When he speaks a lie, he speaks from his own resources,** for he is a liar and the father of it* (John 8:44).

If you want further insight in to why God would allow this, we need to go to the Scriptures. The Bible gives us a way we can look at what God does outside the Scripture as long as it confirms Scripture. This is by looking at the natural order.

> *because what may be known of God is manifest in them, for God has shown it to them. For since the creation of the world His invisible attributes are clearly seen, being understood by*

the things that are made, even His eternal power and God-head, so that they are without excuse . . . (Romans 1:19-20).

In the natural order God has created the predator and the prey. According to the natural order predators eat the prey typically by seeking out the weak and the vulnerable. When the weak are singled out they are targeted for food. This process in the end provides for a healthy gene pool for reproduction and also holds in check over population. The natural order is delicately balanced through this process. Now the devil does not prey on people to destroy the weak and vulnerable. As a matter of fact God calls the weak and vulnerable to bring glory to His honor and strength.

*For you see your calling, brethren, that not many wise according to the flesh, not many mighty, not many noble, are called. But God has chosen the foolish things of the world to put to shame the wise, and **God has chosen the weak things of the world** to put to shame the things which are mighty . . .* (1 Corinthians 1:26-27).

The devil then becomes God's tool to reveal the weaknesses of the called out ones so they can deal with their weakness through the power of God. This predator/prey principle is illustrated in the Scripture in 1 Peter 5:8. Here we see God is not trying to eliminate weak people but individual weaknesses so we can become stronger as a person.

Be sober, be vigilant; because your adversary the devil walks about like a roaring lion, seeking whom he may devour. Resist him, steadfast in the faith, knowing that the same sufferings are experienced by your brotherhood in the world (1 Peter 5:8-9).

The devil goes about as a roaring lion. This is a significant concept. In the African plains there is a perpetual struggle between the beasts of prey and the predators. The lions are a good example of how predation works. Typically the male lion does not actively participate in the kill but is sure to be first in line for dinner. What often happens is the male lends itself through making a roar and being visible so the prey animals will be overcome by fear and do what comes naturally run. The pride of females will in turn form a trap for them to run into so they can be taken by surprise, overcome by fear, and without a proper avoidance mechanism at work be captured. The devil will use the same tactic. He will use the roar or sound of his voice through situations and circumstances to cause us to respond out of fear or some other irrational emotion. The devil's device will cause us to operate in a carnal manner and not in faith and we will easily become victims of the circumstances of life. Our strongest defense is to resist him by operating in the realm of faith knowing that the control of our life is ultimately in God's hands when we put it there!

To see how this process works in us let's go back to the story of Genesis. After man has sinned God comes calling for them. When they acknowledge what they have done God pronounces His judgment in the matter. To the serpent He says:

> *"Because you have done this, You are cursed more than all cattle. And more than every beast of the field; On your belly you shall go. And **you shall eat dust All the days of your life. And I will put enmity Between you and the woman,** And between **your seed and her Seed; He shall bruise your head, And you shall bruise His heel"** (Genesis 3:14-15).*

Now we know snakes do not eat dust and we have surmised this is not a literal snake. The devil, however, does live on the dust of the human experience. When God created man He created us from the dust of the earth. This represents the flesh part of who we are. The position of the devil is to live from the dust or flesh works of man. It is no coincidence that the temptation in the garden is the temptation of the flesh also called the "world."

> *Do not love the world or the things in the world. If anyone loves the world, the love of the Father is not in him. For all*

> *that is in the world—**the lust of the flesh**, the **lust of the eyes**,*
> *and the **pride of life**—is not of the Father but is of the world*
> *(1 John 2:15-16).*

Note this is the threefold temptation in the Garden.

> *So when the woman saw that the tree was **good for food**,*
> *(LUST OF THE FLESH) that it was **pleasant to the eyes**,*
> *(LUST OF THE EYES) and a **tree desirable to make one***
> ***wise**, (PRIDE OF LIFE) she took of its fruit and ate. She also*
> *gave to her husband with her, and he ate (Genesis 3:6).*

When the serpent enticed the woman she was enticed with
the world. We face a different world than she did in her primitive
garden, but though the things of the world change the underlying
principles are the same and so are the roots of temptation. Because
he tempted mankind with their flesh desires, this would now become the devil's food. This also becomes the door for his power. He
lives in the vacuum of human weakness. It is human weakness that
provides his opportunity and it is our willingness to turn to God
that defeats him. Remember when Jesus Christ was going to the
cross, He said the god of the age had come to Him. Why didn't the
devil have power over Him?

> *I will no longer talk much with you, for the ruler of this world*
> *is coming, and he has nothing in Me (John 14:30).*

In the Garden of Gethsemane Jesus had faced His own resistance to the will of the Father. Once He had surrendered to the
will of the Father, there was nothing in Him for the devil to feed on.
Not only was it necessary to settle His heart before the Father, but
He also had to put the people around Him in their place when they
tried to get Him to resist the will of the Father. Remember when
Peter tried to tell Jesus he wouldn't let Him go to the cross? How
did Jesus respond to him?

Then Peter took Him aside and began to rebuke Him, saying, "Far be it from You, Lord; this shall not happen to You!" But He turned and said to Peter, "Get behind Me, Satan! You are an offense to Me, for you are not mindful of the things of God, but the things of men" (Matthew 16:22-23).

Sometimes the devil will come as a serpent; sometimes he will come through our loved ones. The way we defeat him is the same.

Therefore submit to God. *Resist the devil and he will flee from you. Draw near to God and He will draw near to you. Cleanse your hands, you sinners; and purify your hearts, you double-minded. Lament and mourn and weep! Let your laughter be turned to mourning and your joy to gloom.* ***Humble yourselves in the sight of the Lord,*** *and He will lift you up* (James 4:7-10).

Sad to say many people have a false notion on how to fight against the devil. We think the devil is afraid of our power displays and high-minded exclamations of ourselves. The word is clear that the path to victory lies in humility not pride. Pride is, in fact, the devil's food. He comes hungry to those types of gatherings and prospers quite well. The book of Jude exhorts us to be careful of this attitude.

Yet Michael the archangel, in contending with the devil, when he disputed about the body of Moses, dared not bring against him a reviling accusation, but said, "The Lord rebuke you!" But these speak evil of whatever they do not know; and whatever they know naturally, like brute beasts, in these things they corrupt themselves (Jude 9-10).

Repentance is the key to defeating the devil. When we confess our sins God is not only faithful to forgive us of our sins but to cleanse us from all unrighteousness. This cleansing is what diminishes the devil's power. Darkness cannot stand before the light. I believe we are living in the time when the church will go forth in great power and demonstration of the Kingdom of God by truly assaulting the power of darkness.

Many times in interpreting Scripture we take what the Bible calls a private interpretation. We should not translate Scripture from our observation or persuasion but we should allow the Word to interpret itself. An example of this pattern of misinterpretation concerns Ananias in the book of Acts. In the early days of the Jewish church, people were selling all and pooling their resources. Ananias and his wife decided to hold back some of their money while making people think they were doing what everybody else was doing. The Apostle Peter responded by challenging them.

> *But Peter said, "Ananias, why has Satan filled your heart to lie to the Holy Spirit and keep back part of the price of the land for yourself?" (Acts 5:3)*

This Scripture could imply satan is the cause of this problem since it says satan filled his heart to lie. However, seen in the context of the whole story Peter says something different to his wife.

> *Then Peter said to her, "How is it that you have agreed together to test the Spirit of the Lord? Look, the feet of those who have buried your husband are at the door, and they will carry you out" (Acts 5:9).*

The root of the problem was not satan but the self-centered intent of the transgressors. This is why the end result is God's judgment upon Ananias and his wife since they alone were responsible for their actions. Satan, obviously, could have influenced them in the justification for their behavior, but the root of the problem was in their heart. We the people of God are often opposing ourselves by our wrong attitudes. This simply gives strength to the devil in our lives. This is why we need to come to our senses and keep ourselves in the right frame of thinking. This will provide us an escape from the power of the enemy.

*And a servant of the Lord must not quarrel but be gentle to all, able to teach, patient, in humility correcting those who are in opposition, if God perhaps will grant **them repentance, so that they may know the truth,** and that they may come to their senses and escape the snare of the devil, having been taken captive by him to do his will* (2 Timothy 2:24-26).

How powerful it can be when we simply bring our human thoughts into the obedience of the Word of God.

For the weapons of our warfare are not carnal but mighty in God for pulling down strongholds, casting down arguments and every high thing that exalts itself against the knowledge of God, bringing every thought into captivity to the obedience of Christ (2 Corinthians 10: 4-5).

The seed of the woman will overcome in this hour. Again, this woman is the church. Her seed is first the Christ Himself who is the forerunner. He was the firstborn among many brethren. The book of Revelation chapter 12 outlines how this power struggle will ensue.

The story begins with a woman garnished in heavenly attire. She has a garnishment on her head of 12 stars. This is the bride of God, the church, called the church in the wilderness when it was the natural seed of Abraham. In this chapter she transitions to the spiritual seed of Christ, Jesus Christ, the firstborn of the resurrection. When He ascends into heaven Jesus brings the victory. There the power of the devil was broken and he was cast down from the heavenly realm with his messengers, not as a fallen angel, but as an instrument of God rendered powerless according to God's planned purpose. No longer in the heavenly realm, the devil has no opportunity to bring his accusations against us before the throne of God. Remember how in the book of Job the devil accused Job before the ensuing battle Job was caught up in? This behavior is no longer tolerated in heaven.

How do we overcome the enemy?

And they overcame him by the blood of the Lamb and by the word of their testimony, and they did not love their lives to the death (Revelation 12:11).

We overcome through the blood of the Lamb. We stand guilt-less before the throne of grace. By our testimony we release the power of the gospel in our lives. But the third level God is taking us to is when we love not our life to the death. When we are fully con-secrated before the Lord we will truly overcome the wicked one and his power will be vanquished! The seed of the women will prevail for the Lord has declared it ahead of time. The devil knows his time is short so now he is going forth with a vengeance. This is why we must fully understand in this hour how to fight the good fight of faith.

The whole of creation groans for the revealing of the sons of God in the earth. Why? They are part of the curse and our deliver-ance will bring forth their deliverance.

For the creation was subjected to futility, not willingly, but because of Him who subjected it in hope; because the creation itself also will be delivered from the bondage of corruption into the glorious liberty of the children of God. For we know that the whole creation groans and labors with birth pangs to-gether until now (Romans 8:20-22).

This explains how the serpent was cursed above all the rest of creation. Everything groans for deliverance except him. He only waits for judgment. No wonder he is so mad!

Chapter Three

THE WILDERNESS

In the beginning God created the natural order with man as His crowning achievement. It is hard for us to fathom that we are the ones God has created to be fruitful, multiply, and fill up the earth. Just think, He is so impressed with us He wants us to fill up the earth. When we survey the human condition it is hard for us to imagine God really has this much confidence in us. I believe much of our theology is based on our skepticism rather than our faith in God and His plan for us. We are like the psalmist who was obviously incredulous of the fact God chose man for such a wonderful place in His plans and purpose.

> When I consider Your heavens, the work of Your fingers, The moon and the stars, which You have ordained, What is man that You are mindful of him, And the son of man that You visit him? For You have made him a little lower than the angels, And You have crowned him with glory and honor. You have made him to have dominion over the works of Your hands; You have put all things under his feet... (Psalm 8:3-6).

It is interesting to me how anti-humankind we are. This is true both in the church and outside the church. I am a fan of nature films and programs that show various aspects of nature. I love the natural order and God's wisdom in its design. When I was a kid I loved animals but wasn't a very good animal owner. When I was young I always wanted my parents to let me have pets. We lived in the country so I would have owned any animal they would have allowed me to own. I remember once my dad got me a Dalmatian dog. It was around the time of the Disney film *101 Dalmatians* so I was especially excited about my pet. One day at dinner my dad asked me how my dog was. I said, "The dog is doing okay. The problem is he has been asleep for several days!" He immediately led us all outside where we discovered the poor dog was frozen solid. Needless to say, I was in the doghouse then, so to speak, and had a hard time convincing my parents or anyone else I loved animals. What I found out is I love animals but wasn't a good caretaker. That's when I decided I needed to be a lover of wild animals because I could enjoy them and they could take care of themselves.

Over the years, I noticed most naturalists had a far different perspective than my own. As I watched nature films, I noticed a general consensus that nature is good until man comes along. We are spoilers of the superior natural order. The cruelty of nature is always explained away by the beautiful balance of nature, but man is always shown as the great destroyer. Ironically, this is the same attitude most Christians have about the plan of God. Everything is beautiful until people come along. In fact many people think their most spiritual moments are when they get away from it all, especially people, and get alone with God. This is why we think God will one day push us aside and get the job done for Himself. After all, how can God do anything with us? In the end we think that if people are involved it will fail. But is this how God feels? Absolutely not! Including us in His plan requires a lot of patience since God has chosen to work through the natural and human condition, but God will be faithful until all He has spoken comes to pass. Jesus said; "I will build my church and the gates of hell will not prevail against it." I believe Him at His Word. How about you?

God has chosen man to overtake the natural order and to domesticate it by stewardship. This is why God planted the first garden and placed man there. From there we are called to conquer the natural order. In other words, God provides the materials and leaves it up to us what we will do with it. We will be judged on what we do with what God has placed in our hands. This is why responsible stewardship of natural resources is absolutely biblical, but it must also be tempered with the fact God has given these things for the benefit of man. The Word of God gives us a very important principle in 1 Corinthians 15:46, that with God it is first the natural then afterward the spiritual. God began the natural order then created man with His own Spirit or breath in us. This God breath makes it possible for us to be spiritual and through our spiritual development conquer the natural side of our human condition. From there we tackle the natural world around us. The natural is not bad it just needs to be subjugated by the spirit. This signifies the major battle is not in the flesh or natural realm but in the spirit realm.

> *For though we walk in the flesh, we do not war according to the flesh. For the weapons of our warfare are not carnal but mighty in God for pulling down strongholds, casting down arguments and every high thing that exalts itself against the knowledge of God, bringing every thought into captivity to the obedience of Christ, and being ready to punish all disobedience when your obedience is fulfilled* (2 Corinthians 10:3-6).

When God placed man in the Garden of Eden he was given a natural responsibility to guard and cultivate the garden. The obstacle in the end was spiritual. They lost the battle in the realm of the spirit when they submitted to the influence of the serpent rather than being obedient to God. If you will notice when the Word declares our need to engage in this spiritual battle we are called to cast down the arguments and thoughts that are contrary to the Word of God. In that sense the battle becomes an internal one because the issue is not what is happening on the outside but on the inside. It is what is on the inside that will lead to our fall.

> *You were perfect in your ways from the day you were created, Till iniquity was found in you. "By the abundance of your trading You became filled with violence within, And you sinned; Therefore I cast you as a profane thing Out of the*

*mountain of God; And I destroyed you, **O covering cherub,** From the midst of the fiery stones"* (Ezekiel 28:15-16).

When speaking of spiritual things we often see this as being only in the realm of the human spirit, the Holy Spirit, or even a false spirit. It is here we often miss the major point of spiritual conflict. When speaking of one's spiritual perception Jesus taught the source of our perception was not the human spirit but the heart. It is this lack of understanding that not only misguides a lot of people in spiritual warfare but is also the source of the loss of victory in this realm.

*Therefore I speak to them in parables, because seeing they do not see, and hearing they do not hear, nor do they understand. And in them the prophecy of Isaiah is fulfilled, which says: 'Hearing you will hear and shall not understand, And seeing you will see and not perceive; **For the hearts of this people have grown dull. Their ears are hard of hearing, And their eyes they have closed,** Lest they should see with their eyes and hear with their ears, Lest they should understand with their hearts and turn, So that I should heal them'* (Matthew 13:13-15).

*When anyone hears the word of the kingdom, and **does not understand it,** then **the wicked one comes and snatches away** what was sown in his heart. This is he who received seed by the wayside* (Matthew 13:19).

True spiritual perception is an issue of the heart. This is why many people miss out on God and do not have spiritual understanding. As noted in the Scriptures, this is the first reason people fail to go forward with God and become a victim of the devil. If this error leads us to external religious observance as a replacement for true spiritual power the devil will probably leave us alone. We are no threat to him. If we pursue the things of the spirit with this mindset and with no understanding of the role of the heart in spiritual perception, we will be religiously bound and not know it. We will seek to go into the spiritual realm to defeat the devil but will by and large be powerless. This is why so many charismatic/Pentecostal Christians have developed such intensive teachings on the devil but in the end have had no real power to overcome him. They make a lot of noise but are never much of a threat to the devil or his kingdom. They think they are spiritual but have no true spiritual perception. The devil is always snatching their seed and they don't know why! You can be filled with the Holy Spirit, manifest the gifts of the Spirit, even have a five-fold ministry, but if your heart is not right your spiritual perception is clouded. No wonder we are always so surprised when gifted people are so carnal! We don't understand what it means to be spiritual.

The Apostle Paul wrote a letter to the Corinthian church and admonished them about their carnal ways and the fact they were just "baby" Christians. Yet when the book of 1 Corinthians opens, he tells them they have all the gifts, knowledge of the Word, and the best of speakers. The charismatic church needs to reassess our lack of power and go back to the foundation of our experience. We need repentance and turning to God with our heart to fully experience the blessing of God. When Jesus Christ came He came to a strong religious system that looked very glorious from the outside but had no true spiritual perception. I believe he would see the same thing if He came to the church today. The church seems so big and powerful but has such little impact on our world. I have also observed that some of the greatest voices in the church are not what we in the charismatic/Pentecostal tradition, would call spirit filled. How can this be? People without the pursuit of spiritual gifts have been in pursuit of God and their pure hearts have given them the ability to see what others do not see. How much more could we do if in our pursuit for God we also developed our spiritual gifts and callings?

Once we establish our battle lines as an internal battle involving the heart then we can understand the place of the devil and how we can overcome him in this day. It is from this perspective we must deal with the concept of the wilderness. Before the children of Israel could enter the Promised Land they had to pass through the wilderness. Before Jesus Christ could begin His ministry He had to conquer the devil in the wilderness. We need to understand that the wilderness is not just an accident but it is a part of the plan of God. It is in the wilderness that we face ourselves and are given the tools to overcome and become the heirs of God. The children of Israel are the first example. They faced many enemies but the lesson was the same. If your heart is right you will overcome, but if your heart is not right you will be overcome and miss the blessings of God. We must learn the lessons of the wilderness.

> *And you shall remember that the LORD your God led you all the way these forty years in the wilderness, to humble you and test you, **to know what was in your heart,** whether you would keep His commandments or not. So **He humbled you, allowed you to hunger,** and fed you with manna which you did not know nor did your fathers know, that He might make you know that man shall not live by bread alone; but man lives by every word that proceeds from the mouth of the LORD* (Deuteronomy 8:2-3).

Jesus Christ was led into the wilderness by the Spirit. Here He would be tempted by the devil. Jesus Christ, like the Israelites before Him, was brought to hunger. In this case Jesus Christ was led to His choice in response to the Holy Spirit through fasting. This was necessary so He could do what Adam, the first man, did not do. He would show us how to resist the devil and overcome in this world. Adam faced the devil in the Garden; again, since the battle is on the inside the circumstances are not the major issue. Adam's response should have been a defensive one so he could keep the command to guard the garden he was cultivating. Jesus wasn't in a garden. He had a different agenda. He was on an offensive mission. His goal was the binding of the strong man so we could make a spoil of his goods. In that sense the children of Israel were on the offense going to the Promised Land. In either case the test would be the same. Jesus, like Adam, would be tested on the lust of the flesh, the lust of the eyes and the pride of life.

The biggest temptation I see the devil offering Jesus is a quicker route to everything the Father would have given. Jesus was on track to become the Lord of everything. It would certainly be true His hunger was temporary and there would be no limits to His power in the end. Jesus would one day be fully recognized as the King of Kings and Lord of Lords. The devil was offering a faster route without the pain and delays the Father's way would lead Him. I think this is why so many people are easily defeated. We often think we are even helping God along by our shortcuts. Efficiency is our goal when God is trying to demonstrate our sufficiency is in Him! In the Garden of Eden access to the knowledge of good and evil would come when they were ready for it. Even now, for the mature, God wants us to be proficient in the understanding and discernment of good and evil.

> *For though by this time you ought to be teachers, you need someone to teach you again the first principles of the oracles of God; and you have come to need milk and not solid food. For everyone who partakes only of milk is unskilled in the word of righteousness, for he is a babe.* **But solid food belongs to those who are of full age,** *that is, those who by reason of use have their* **senses exercised to discern both good and evil** (Hebrews 5:12-14).

After Jesus resisted the devil the devil left Him. If there is no opening in your heart the devil is powerless and you are powerful. From this point Jesus Christ began to preach, "Repent for the kingdom of heaven is at hand." When the devil is defeated the Kingdom of God is extended to the boundary of his resistance.

> *But if I cast out demons with the finger of God , surely the kingdom of God has come upon you. When a strong man, fully armed, guards his own palace, his goods are in peace. But when a stronger than he comes upon him and overcomes him, he takes from him all his armor in which he trusted, and divides his spoils* (Luke 11:20-22).

When we really understand this principle we will also be great messengers of the Kingdom of God. We will be those who extend this reign on the earth. This is the picture we see in the beginning. God's appointed man is in the garden God has given for his stewardship. Surrounding the garden is the howling wilderness. As we are first faithful in our garden we can then be active in extending the reign of the kingdom. Those who have the power with the announcement are those who have overcome the wicked one. Jesus Christ is our example. From His position of authority, in the kingdom, Jesus Christ had power over the darkness.

> *And Jesus went about all Galilee, teaching in their synagogues, preaching the gospel of the kingdom, and healing all kinds of sickness and all kinds of disease among the people. Then His fame went throughout all Syria; and they brought to Him all sick people who were afflicted with various diseases and torments, and those who were demon-possessed, epileptics, and paralytics; and He healed them* (Matthew 4:23-24).

This is just the opposite influence of the first man, Adam. When confronted with the temptation of the serpent, man fell victim to his own passion and desire. This choice not only alienated him from God but also loosed the power of darkness. The prince of the power of the air was loosed with his habitation being all disobedience of man, uncontrolled desires, and the inclination to walk in the flesh or natural realm rather than the realm of God.

> *...in which you once walked according to the course of this world, according to the prince of the power of the air, the spirit who now works in the sons of disobedience, among whom also we all once conducted ourselves in the lusts of our flesh, fulfilling the desires of the flesh and of the mind, and were by nature children of wrath, just as the others* (Ephesians 2:2-3).

We are born into this web of spiritual wickedness through the choice of Adam. Through one man death entered the world. Thank

God from one man, Jesus Christ, came the reversal of Adam's choice. We need to be reconciled to God but also recognize how we are commissioned to break the power of the devil in our lives and to loose the world around us from this curse. It is time now to reverse the curse and walk in the kingdom and power of the Christ!

Chapter Four

Spiritual Warfare

There is much written these days concerning spiritual warfare. My desire is that you not be offended but that you be challenged to reassess your thinking based upon the Word of God. As with many issues concerning the devil and the power of darkness, a lot of concepts practiced by Christians are based more on superstition than the Word of God. Jesus said something very telling to His contemporaries. Jesus said, "wisdom is justified by her children." In other words, what are the results of your doctrine? Is your doctrine really producing long term results? Are you willing to re-examine things you have practiced over time for their productivity or will you in your pride hold on to unscriptural notions? When you have practiced a certain doctrine for many years it takes a great deal of humility to lay it down when confronted with reality. Unfortunately, it is our pride that has given the enemy such a foothold in our world. Keeping your mind open, let's examine the Scriptures.

The Apostle Paul speaks about spiritual warfare in the book of Ephesians chapter 6.

> *Finally, my brethren, be strong in the Lord and in the power of His might. Put on the whole armor of God, that you may be able to stand against the wiles of the devil. For we do not wrestle against flesh and blood, but against principalities, against powers, against the rulers of the darkness of this age, against spiritual hosts of wickedness in the heavenly places* (Ephesians 6:10-12).

We certainly need to be aware of the fact we are living in a world where there is more going on than meets the human eye. There is a spiritual realm we need to be aware of consisting of both the light and the darkness. We need this perception of the spiritual realm if we are going to fulfill the purpose God has for us. I believe as the final days of history unfold, the spiritual realm will become more real to the church not less. We must recognize that the need for too much information was the problem in the beginning as it may well be today. Often people will take a doctrine and fill in the blanks with all kinds of suppositions based not on the Word but their own observations and expectations. This has been especially true when it comes to spiritual warfare. The other problem is our desire to take control of our lives and the events surrounding our life. A good example is the interpretation of the experience the prophet Daniel had. In Daniel chapter 10 we read that one day he was seeking the Lord for spiritual understanding. After several days he received an angelic visitation. The angel told him he was detained by the prince of Persia but after he received help he was able to complete his journey. This scene could certainly refer to the principalities and powers of heavenly places, but do we have license to put together a doctrine where it then becomes our job to intervene in this spiritual conflict? The angel did not tell Daniel the situation would have been expedited by his participation in this spiritual conflict, but many people have assumed that to be true. What biblical basis does this insight into the spiritual realm give us that prompts us to believe God wants us to participate in His affairs?

Daniel had been fasting and praying and the angel informed him God had heard and sent the answer to his prayer immediately. The fact he explained the situation to Daniel did not invite him to become involved. Daniel was a prophet. Prophets are seers. This means they can see what other people cannot see. One of the signs of maturity is our ability to hold information without trying to take charge of the situation. Many times a prophet has information from God they are not supposed to act upon. In the book of Acts the prophet Agabus binds his own hands and feet with Paul's belt to demonstrate what will happen to Paul if he goes to Jerusalem.

He warns him not to go. Paul, on the other hand, knows he is not only supposed to go, but is prepared both to suffer and die for the kingdom. Why did Paul feel this way? Paul knew the will and purpose of God for his life and he did in fact become a martyr for the Kingdom of God. How sad that in the Charismatic-Pentecostal Movement we have so many people who are trying to take control of situations they do not have the insight to fully understand. Just like Ananias, we see in this story of Paul, we can be motivated by our fears rather than our faith and confidence in the Almighty God.

When looking at what the Apostle Paul calls the weapons of our warfare you will note most of the equipment is for the purpose of self-defense. This defensive equipment again has to do with what we do to prepare ourselves not what we do against the enemy.

> *Stand therefore, having girded your waist **with truth**, having put on the breastplate of **righteousness**, and having shod your feet with the preparation of the **gospel of peace**; above all, taking the **shield of faith** with which you will be able to quench all the fiery darts of the wicked one. And take the **helmet of salvation**, and the **sword of the Spirit**, which is the word of God . . . (Ephesians 6:14-17).*

There are several keys to understanding the weapons of our warfare. Truth is where it all begins. God wants us to maintain our integrity and to stay honest before Him and our fellow man. Can you imagine how much trouble would be avoided in life if we just stayed open and honest? In the end dark motivations will always result in dark actions. The devil's biggest tool is deception. Shouldn't we immediately recognize this as an opening for the evil one when we are walking in his character rather than the character of God? Because the Jews did not have a love for the truth Jesus told them they were like their father, the devil, who was a liar from the beginning. John in his revelation shows an overcoming company with the Lamb on the mountain of the Lord who could sing the new song. Why could they stand with the Lamb?

> *These are the ones who were not defiled with women, for they are virgins. These are the ones who follow the Lamb wherever He goes. These were redeemed from among men, being first-fruits to God and to the Lamb. And in their mouth was found no deceit, for they are without fault before the throne of God* (Revelation 14:4-5).

These who are the cream of the crop have no guile or deception in them. As virgins they represent those who practice righteousness even in the secret place.

The second key to victory is the breastplate of righteousness. Righteousness is from the root word sampling meaning doing what is right. Doing the right thing is not always easy but in the end it will produce positive results. The enemy hates righteousness. His power comes when we rebel against God. As with Jesus Christ Himself, the devil must flee from us when we resist him by doing what is right. Righteousness in the Scripture not only speaks of doing right but speaks of the state of the believer who is fully cleansed by the power of Christ through the blood of the Lamb. The devil, whose name means accuser, used shame and condemnation to bring us into his snare. When discussing the fall of the dragon from heaven we see the blood of the ascended Lamb made the dragon's accusations powerless. In the Old Testament Job was accused by satan of only serving God because of how good life was going for him. The ensuing conflict was the test Job endured to prove this accusation as untrue. The New Testament Christian does not have to prove our righteousness for it is only fully found in Christ. Never allow yourself to be brought into this snare but use the Word of God to declare:

> *There is therefore now no condemnation to those who are in Christ Jesus, who do not walk according to the flesh, but according to the Spirit. For the law of the Spirit of life in Christ Jesus has made me free from the law of sin and death. For what the law could not do in that it was weak through the flesh, God did by sending His own Son in the likeness of sinful flesh, on account of sin: He condemned sin in the flesh,*

that the righteous requirement of the law might be fulfilled in us who do not walk according to the flesh but according to the Spirit (Romans 8:1-4).

Please note the stipulation is "to those who are walking according to the Spirit and not according to the flesh." We must be girded with truth in the sense we are honestly trying to live righteously before God. Our slogan should always be "do your best so God can do the rest."

Sow for yourselves righteousness; Reap in mercy; Break up your fallow ground, For it is time to seek the LORD, Till He comes and rains righteousness on you (Hosea 10:12).

Condemnation is difficult to deal with and the devil is always dishing it out. This is why the Revelation says the seed of the woman will overcome by the blood of the Lamb. Through the blood of Jesus we have complete forgiveness of sin. If we confess our sin He is faithful to forgive us and to cleanse us from all unrighteousness. It is like the story of Joshua in the book of Zechariah chapter 3. Joshua was standing before the Angel of the Lord and satan was standing next to him in opposition. The Lord rebuked him and then gave Joshua a new set of clothes. The "new clothes" represent the righteousness of the saints who have been made clean by the blood of the Lamb. The cleansing God gives makes the devil powerless to accuse us.

This is why the chronology of the book of Revelations 12 is so important. Many people see the devil as a fallen angel cast out of heaven before the creation. This is not true. The devil is cast out of heaven when Jesus Christ ascended to heaven with His blood as the purchase price for our redemption. After this great act of love on our behalf the devil, or satan, can no longer oppose us before God with accusations. This is our great salvation that becomes our helmet of defense.

"Then I heard a loud voice saying in heaven, 'Now salvation, and strength, and the kingdom of our God, and the power of

His Christ have come, for the accuser of our brethren, who accused them before our God day and night, has been cast down. And they overcame him by the blood of the Lamb and by the word of their testimony, and they did not love their lives to the death'" (Revelation 12:10).

As it was in the story of Job, before this event satan could make accusations against us even going before the throne. Not any more!

The third key is to have "the gospel of peace." The Bible says, "follow peace with all men and holiness without which we cannot see God." It goes on to say, "least a root of bitterness springing up cause trouble and by this many become defiled." Have you noticed how many Christians have been sidelined through holding things against other people? The enemy is very good at giving us reasons for our grudges we bear. The problem with this way of thinking is we never benefit from this reasoning. Instead in the end we are robbed of our peace and as a result we suffer.

The spiritual weapon here is the gospel or good news of forgiveness. Jesus tells the story of a man who was forgiven much in Matthew 18. This man owed his master a lot of money and so the master commanded he be sold with his family to pay his debt. He cried out to the master for mercy and it was granted. Time passes and later this man faced the same dilemma except that he was the one who had the power to forgive the debt. Much less money was involved and yet his response was to not have mercy. When the former master heard of this he had the man turned over to the torturers. Of course, the first analogy is our need to forgive others in light of what God has forgiven us for. But we also see the end result of unforgiveness is to be turned over to the torturers. This follows the pattern of the Scripture that says when we allow ourselves to violate the principles of the Word of God we open ourselves up to the tormentor, the devil, who will willingly help us pay the price for our sin. Often times these tormented people will seek counseling and consolation and many will offer it, but they will never find a cure for their malady except simple forgiveness.

The fourth key is the shield of faith. This shield will quench the fires of the wicked one. Note what this means. We will not have to go on the defense when we trust in God. Our faith is our defense. From this position we can walk in confidence and also rest. I have met so many people who in their constant vigilance against the devil never seem to be able to enter the rest of God. They are always looking over their shoulder or speculating that the enemy is at work. For them the enemy is an unrestrained predator. They must keep a constant guard not on their heart but on a lurking enemy who they feel can actually do bad things to them without God's knowledge or consent. Remember when satan came before God concerning Job? He had to ask for consent to receive the freedom to test Job. Jesus, Himself was led into the wilderness by the Holy Spirit to be tempted of the devil and as mentioned Jesus Christ told Peter, "satan has desired to test you but I have prayed for you." This doesn't sound like a freewheeling conflict but a very controlled one with God at the helm. When the children of Israel came to the Promised Land they were waylaid by the enemy they faced. The book of Hebrews tells us the problem was a lack of faith.

> *Therefore, since a promise remains of entering His rest, let us fear lest any of you seem to have come short of it. For indeed the gospel was preached to us as well as to them; but the word which they heard did not profit them, not being mixed with faith in those who heard it. For we who have believed do enter that rest, as He has said: "So I swore in My wrath, 'They shall not enter My rest,'" although the works were finished from the foundation of the world* (Hebrews 4:1-3).

Not only should we avoid a warfare mentality, but we should always move with the confidence God's work was finished from the foundation of the world. We are going after the promises settled before the foundation of the world. Although like the children of Israel there is an enemy to overcome, we must move forward with a sense of a victory already accomplished. Everything was officially settled before the foundation of the world, and we need to see that

47

the failure we seemingly brought to the plan was fully eliminated when Jesus died on the Cross. His words need to always ring true in our minds.

> *So when Jesus had received the sour wine, He said, "It is finished!" And bowing His head, He gave up His spirit* (John 19:30).

The children of Israel thought they were trying to take a land. God wanted them to see the possibility of receiving something powerful from Him. God wanted them to have such a confidence of faith in God they would know whatever problem they faced God was able to give them the victory. In this place we will be in a position of rest where we will never respond emotionally out of fear, but we will confidently stand till the victory has been won. This steadfastness will put the "roaring lion" off guard.

I was watching a nature film about cheetahs in the wild of Africa. They are predators who, like the lion, chase prey who run in fear of them. Something was wrong with the gazelle the cheetah had singled out and it did not run from the cheetah. When the gazelle failed to run the cheetah was taken off guard and was unable to attack the gazelle. It stopped dead in its tracks and was unable to function. It actually swatted the gazelle to get it to run, but when the gazelle failed to respond the cheetah finally walked away. I see that as an example of what will happen to the church that is strong in faith and unflinching in the face of adversity. The devil may swat at us but will be powerless when we fail to respond in fear.

The fifth key is the helmet of salvation. The word salvation in the Scriptures means much more than we have recognized. It means deliverance and is typified in the Scriptures by the story of the children of Israel. They were in the bondage of Egypt and God wanted to bring them out and then take them to the Promised Land. God wants to take us out of bondage and take us in to the fullness of the inheritance He has for our life. Salvation is not just an insurance policy against hell but much more. If salvation is deliverance we must be fully delivered from the sins that have us bound. Before the children of Israel could enter into the Promised Land they needed to get Egypt out of them not just get them out of Egypt. This is why God took them through the wilderness. He took them through the wilderness to show them what was in their heart. Through this process they could see what was on the inside and get rid of it. When they finished the wilderness process they would not only be further along in their journey, but they would be ready for the Promised Land.

In Joshua chapter five God stopped them and required them to renew themselves fully in the covenant before they could go forward. This required the renewing of the covenant of circumcision. Living under the reproach of Egypt, they were always struggling about whether to go forward or to go back. Those people who had not been fully delivered from their past were always struggling to go back. This inward inclination to turn back gives the enemy a lot of power over us. I will deal with this issue more fully in other chapters, but we need to settle an important issue in our minds. When the devil tempted Jesus in the wilderness his major jab was "if you are the Son of God" do such and such. Jesus was not moved by these temptations because He knew where He came from, who He was, and where He was going. How about you? Do you know who you are or are you still struggling with your identity in Christ?

Finally, comes our one offensive weapon, the sword of the spirit, which is the Word of God. Here Paul asks for prayers that utterance might be given him for the furtherance of the gospel. The word in the Scripture here is the "rhema" or spoken Word of God. The letter of the Word will not be effective in this spiritual struggle. The devil and his minions know the Word probably better than most Christians. The devil used the Word against Jesus in the wilderness. Paul said he came not with enticing words of men's wisdom but in the power and demonstration of the Word of God. We must understand that the Word receives its power when it is anointed by the Spirit of God. The anointing gives the Word life. In this day we must declare the Word of God in the power of the anointing not just with logical persuasion so common in the church today.

Teaching is important for the church. It helps people understand the plans and the purpose of God to bring us to a place of maturity and to equip us to be used for His service, but we need more than understanding to extend the Kingdom of God. We need the power that comes with the anointing. The anointed Word will break the yoke of bondage on the people and release them from everything that binds. It is this Word that will produce the powerful demonstrations necessary to confirm the Word to the unbeliever.

Paul was called to preach the gospel. It is very important we understand what the gospel is if we are to win the spiritual struggle of the ages. The evangelical church has narrowed down the gospel message and in turn has diluted its power. The gospel, or good news as it should properly be translated, is not just Jesus died for our sins so we could be forgiven and go to heaven. The gospel, or good news, is the message of the Kingdom of God. Jesus said; "repent for the Kingdom of God is at hand." The good news is the announcement of the reign of God.

> *How beautiful upon the mountains Are the feet of him who brings good news, Who proclaims peace, Who brings glad tidings of good things, Who proclaims salvation, Who says to Zion, "Your God reigns!"* (Isaiah 52:7)

It is only through this paradigm we can confront the world and the god of this world. We must be fully confident that in the end all things are within the framework of the will of God. We must also be confident we are His instruments called to walk in His Kingdom and that we will be used as His instruments to fully establish His reign in our lives and in the world. This "good news" alone will equip us to walk in the confidence and peace we need to navigate the difficult waters of life.

What is the role of prayer? Paul said to pray that utterance might be given him. Warfare prayer should be directed to seeking God not fighting the enemy. When you see God is the Almighty God you will seek Him for the victory. Do not waste time trying to take it from the enemy. It is not the enemies land to give or surrender. The land is ours to take when God gives it. Prayer is a strange thing. God wants to give us things but He wants us to seek for it. If we don't ask it will not be given.

You lust and do not have. You murder and covet and cannot obtain. You fight and war. Yet you do not have because you do not ask (James 4:3).

This is what God spoke to Joshua. The same principles God spoke to Joshua fully embrace the spiritual walk we are on today.

Every place that the sole of your foot will tread upon I have given you, as I said to Moses. From the wilderness and this Lebanon as far as the great river, the River Euphrates, all the land of the Hittites, and to the Great Sea toward the going down of the sun, shall be your territory. No man shall be able to stand before you all the days of your life; as I was with Moses, so I will be with you. I will not leave you nor forsake you (Joshua 1:3-5).

The book of the Revelation reveals the conflict of the ages and our ultimate victory in the end. In chapter 8 we see the important place of prayer in this struggle.

Then another angel, having a golden censer, came and stood at the altar. He was given much incense, that he should offer it with the prayers of all the saints upon the golden altar which was before the throne. And the smoke of the incense, with the prayers of the saints, ascended before God from the angel's hand. Then the angel took the censer, filled it with fire from the altar, and threw it to the earth. And there were noises, thunderings, lightnings, and an earthquake (Revelation 8:3-5).

The prayers of the saints are what release the judgments of God. The Revelation corresponds to the book of Job in that the people of God are caught up in a great struggle without full understanding of the events. Although not fully appraised of what is happening, the events purge and purify them as their prayers and even groanings produce supernatural spiritual power released upon the nations and ultimately the enemy. This demonstrates the power of praying in the Holy Spirit. We do not always understand what we are praying, but our prayers are an important ingredient in attaining the victory. It is too bad in the charismatic, Pentecostal churches we have abandoned this power because we do not see its impact. Even when people pray "in the spirit" they often do so with the end result being "getting in the flesh" by operating in human understanding and motivation rather than being encouraged to go God's way. We end up trying to manage God and our circumstances rather than submitting to God and letting our path be directed by Him. It is time for us to enter into the Kingdom of God and lend ourselves to His will in our prayers. This is true spiritual warfare!

Chapter Five

THE ANOINTED CHERUB

E zekiel chapter 28 is a very important chapter in the study of the devil. It is the chapter many people believe to be the story of the devil's fall from heaven. They believe the devil to be a fallen angel, although, the only scriptural basis one can find is if you apply these Scriptures to that belief. I want to examine this chapter in light of the Scripture so we can more fully understand this important chapter and also understand our place in the plans and purposes of God. I believe Scripture bears out this to be the story of the fall of man **not** the fall of an angel called Lucifer.

First note that verse two tells us that this is a prophecy about the fall and judgment of a man who is the King of Tyre. The allegorical picture of this chapter is relating the true spiritual principles we need to understand. When speaking of the fall of this king the picture alludes to the fall of another person. This person is clearly Adam, the first man.

First this person is said to be the seal of perfection and beauty, full of wisdom and perfect in beauty. Adam was created in the image and likeness of God. What creature could be more perfect than one created in the image and likeness of God? As I already have mentioned, I believe we fail to understand the awesome creature God created when He created man. This creature, man, would be the crowning of the creation and would become His sons in the earth. This creature is collectively pictured as His bride. When reading prophetic books it is very easy to see the beauty God has bestowed upon man and also how God extols us as His chosen vessels of love.

The person spoken of in Ezekiel 28 was in Eden, the garden of God. How can this be anyone other than Adam? Gen 2:8 tells us God planted the Garden of Eden and then He put the man He had created there. The Garden of Eden was not a pre-Adam creation but was planted specifically for Adam. After God placed Adam there, God instructed him to guard and cultivate the garden. Ezekiel calls this guardian a "covering cherub." This means one who is anointed to guard and protect something. This is consistent with the biblical narrative concerning Adam who was created to protect what God had placed in his care. The picture of it as a place where God dwelt is consistent again with the biblical narrative of the garden. After they had sinned it says Adam and Eve; "heard the voice of the Lord walking in the garden in the cool of the day." The Bible also says, "in the garden every precious stone was your covering." I once heard someone say this was not the Garden of Eden because it was a mineral garden not a garden of trees and plants. Yet when someone considers the prophetic imagery used one can see from a scriptural point of view the use of precious stones represents the beauty of divine handiwork. When God does a work in us it is described as the process of making precious stones.

> *"O you afflicted one, Tossed with tempest, and not comforted, Behold, I will lay your stones with colorful gems, And lay your foundations with sapphires. I will make your pinnacles of rubies, Your gates of crystal, And all your walls of precious stones. All your children shall be taught by the LORD, And great shall be the peace of your children"* (Isaiah 54:11-13).

"You were perfect in your ways from the day you were created till iniquity was found in you," Ezekiel 28:15 says. As mentioned in an earlier chapter, Jesus told the people the devil was a liar from the beginning. God had created man as a creature perfectly created in his image and likeness. Everything was good until iniquity or rebellion against the goodness of God was manifested. When inner conflict came as a result of the temptation to disobey God the result was sin or transgressing the law of God. What happened next?

Man was kicked out of the Garden of Eden, separated from the presence of God, and separated from the stewardship God had entrusted them with. This was also the sin of the King of Tyre and it is, indeed, the story of man throughout history. The King of Tyre lost his stewardship by divine judgment. This is, unfortunately, a story told time and time again both in human history and Christian history. The reason this insight about who this chapter is about is so important is because of the major importance of the concept of stewardship in the plans and purposes of God. Everything both in heaven and in earth belongs to God. This was the story and principle God demonstrated in the great reign of Babylon through the ministry of the prophet Daniel.

> *"This decision is by the decree of the watchers, And the sentence by the word of the holy ones, In order that the living may know That the Most High rules in the kingdom of men, Gives it to whomever He will, And sets over it the lowest of men"* (Daniel 4:17).

This important principle of stewardship is essential in understanding our conflict with the devil. The devil only has designated realms in which he can function. We can defeat him through indirect means. When we are faithful to God in our stewardship we disarm the devil and open the doors for divine blessing. As stated here in Daniel, there is a whole spiritual realm that exists, but it's reality shifts and changes based upon the actions in the natural realm. It is the realm of man who was created in the image and likeness of God and empowered to take dominion of the earth that supersedes and controls the spiritual realm not the opposite!

With this understanding we can glean the more important truths of the prophetic books. It will especially open up the book of the Revelation that describes the final stages of the eternal conflict. In Revelation 12:9 we learn the serpent of old is also a dragon. As the serpent he tempts us individually. As the dragon his focus is systems or beasts as John the apostle described those who by worshiping the dragon gave authority to the beast.

> So they worshiped the dragon who gave authority to the
> beast; and they worshiped the beast, saying, "Who is like the
> beast? Who is able to make war with him?" (Revelation 13:4)

This understanding of the devil as a dragon gives illumination
as to why the devil is so rarely mentioned in the Old Testament.
Since he inhabits systems of men the end result becomes the judgment upon the system that he inhabits. Most often the choices people make are not individual but a part of a corporate influence upon
them. It is through these corporate systems the devil yields his greatest influence and we must understand this if we are to defeat him.
These bigger influences can be political systems, cultural influences,
ethnic influences, religious mindsets or traditions, and even economic systems. In these days it is very incumbent that we are able
to walk with wisdom in a higher realm so the Kingdom of God can
advance in the earth. As we approach this important level of understanding, we must still acknowledge God's sovereign reign over
all things and recognize ultimately that all authority comes from
Him. This tells us in our dealings with the devil that we need to
deal with the underlying principles of his power more than we actually need to directly address his role.

In Daniel 10 we read about Daniel seeking the Lord and God
sending an answer by way of the angel Gabriel. When Gabriel gets
to Daniel he explains what was happening behind the scenes in the
spiritual realm.

> Then he said to me, "Do not fear, Daniel, for from the first
> day that you set your heart to understand, and to humble
> yourself before your God, your words were heard; and I have
> come because of your words. But the prince of the kingdom of
> Persia withstood me twenty-one days; and behold, Michael,
> one of the chief princes, came to help me, for I had been left
> alone there with the kings of Persia. Now I have come to make
> you understand what will happen to your people in the lat-
> ter days, for the vision refers to many days yet to come"
> (Daniel 10:12-14).

As I mentioned in an earlier chapter this inspires many people to get involved in the realm of the spiritual struggle, yet, Daniel himself did not feel so compelled. Why? His power came through his prayer and supplication to God who is the Almighty in all these affairs. When John sees in his revelation the spiritual behind the natural events, what he saw was not to provoke us to get involved but to get us to a place of repentance so we can break the source of this problem! The Revelation reveals these systems as the habitation of the dragon, but the way we deal with the issues is still the same.

In Revelation 13 John sees the dragon and his beasts and announces limited authority has been given. The dragon gives his power to the beastly systems; yet, his authority is restricted by the heavenly court. Look at the authority given:

And he was given a mouth speaking great things and blasphemies, and he was given authority to continue for forty-two months. Then he opened his mouth in blasphemy against God, to blaspheme His name, His tabernacle, and those who dwell in heaven. It was granted to him to make war with the saints and to overcome them. And authority was given him over every tribe, tongue, and nation. All who dwell on the earth will worship him, whose names have not been written in the Book of Life of the Lamb slain from the foundation of the world (Revelation 13:5-8).

This same prophetic picture is spoken of in the book of Daniel chapter 7. The difference is this chapter gives insight into the full channel of authority. Daniel mentions the Ancient of Days seated on His throne overseeing the matter. When the Ancient of Days, the Almighty God, makes a decision all power is moved by His judgment.

"I was watching; and the same horn was making war against the saints, and prevailing against them, until the Ancient of Days came, and a judgment was made in favor of the saints

of the Most High, and the time came for the saints to possess the kingdom" (Daniel 7:21-22).

He shall speak pompous words against the Most High, Shall persecute the saints of the Most High, And shall intend to change times and law. Then the saints shall be given into his hand For a time and times and half a time. 'But the court shall be seated, And they shall take away his dominion, To consume and destroy it forever (Daniel 7:25-26).

Now it is very important to note the timing of this judgment. This judgment in favor of the saints is given at the time of the resurrection of Jesus Christ when through His sacrifice He purchased both our freedom and our authority.

"I was watching in the night visions, And behold, One like the Son of Man, Coming with the clouds of heaven! He came to the Ancient of Days, And they brought Him near before Him. Then to Him was given dominion and glory and a kingdom, That all peoples, nations, and languages should serve Him. His dominion is an everlasting dominion, Which shall not pass away, And His kingdom the one Which shall not be destroyed" (Daniel 7:13-14).

When observing the conflict of the earth we, the people of God, must look from the viewpoint of the victorious ones! The devil and all his beasts are under divine judgment. Now it is time for the saints to possess the kingdom.

Then the kingdom and dominion, And the greatness of the kingdoms under the whole heaven, Shall be given to the people, the saints of the Most High. His kingdom is an everlasting kingdom, And all dominions shall serve and obey Him (Daniel 7:27).

Every tribe, nation, and people who live outside God have been given into the hands of the dragon until the time when the saints arise in power and dominion as God has purposed from the beginning of time. The world does not live in the freedom possible for the saints of the Most High God. The world has given themselves over to the beast and without even knowing it are, in fact, worshipping the dragon. Everyone worships the dragon and his systems except the redeemed whose names are in God's book.

> *All who dwell on the earth will worship him, whose names have not been written in the* Book of Life of the Lamb *slain from the foundation of the world* (Revelation 13:8).

But as it was in the beginning so it is true today. The power of the dragon and his beasts does not lie within them but is the result of improper stewardship. Note what John saw about the name of the great economic beast.

> *He causes all, both small and great, rich and poor, free and slave, to receive a mark on their right hand or on their foreheads, and that no one may buy or sell except one who has the mark or the name of the beast, or the number of his name. Here is wisdom. Let him who has understanding calculate the number of the beast, for it is the number of a man: His number is 666* (Revelation 13:16-18).

The NIV says it is a man's number. This Scripture is not trying to tease us with the name of a future mystery man but to inform us the beast and the dragon draw their power from man's disobedience. Our sins and weakness are the fuel of the enemy and when the fuel dries up so will his power! This beast requires his mark to be on the forehead and the hand of every person. This is a direct reference to the scriptural command given to the children of Israel as they entered into the Promised Land. They were told to put the Word of God on their forehead and their hands as frontlets to remind them to always live by the Word. To have the mark of man means to live with human wisdom and understanding outside the mind and will of God. These people stand in startling contrast to the redeemed in Revelation 14 who have the mark of God on their fore-heads and follow the Lamb wherever he leads them.

> *Then I looked, and behold, a Lamb standing on Mount Zion, and with Him one hundred and forty-four thousand, having His Father's name written on their foreheads. They sang as it were a new song before the throne, before the four living crea-tures, and the elders; and no one could learn that song except the hundred and forty-four thousand who were redeemed from the earth. These are the ones who were not defiled with women, for they are virgins. These are the ones who follow the Lamb wherever He goes. These were redeemed from among men, being firstfruits to God and to the Lamb. And in their mouth was found no deceit, for they are without fault before the throne of God (Revelation 14:1, 3-5).*

This overcoming company will indeed defeat the devil by their righteousness. They have been made clean by the blood of the Lamb and secondly by maintaining the purity of their love for God. These will go forth with great power after standing before the throne of God and being empowered to take the everlasting gospel to the nations. Remember Paul's prayer request: "and pray for me that utterance might be given." We, the church of the Lord Jesus Christ, need to see the power of the proclamation of the gospel anointed by the power of the Holy Spirit coming from a people sanctified for their master's use.

The question then becomes why would we need to see the devil behind these things if we are not dealing directly with him in our response? First, God wants us to see how dark the darkness is. The choice we have is not just will I serve God or not but who will I serve? If you are not serving God your self-serving ways will always sell you into a bondage you will have no control over.

> *What then? Shall we sin because we are not under law but under grace? Certainly not! Do you not know that to whom you present yourselves slaves to obey, you are that one's slaves*

whom you obey, whether of sin leading to death, or of obedience leading to righteousness? (Romans 6:15-16)

Independence from God is not freedom but bondage. When we choose to live outside the will and purpose of God we have chosen to live in a dark and foreboding land filled with all manner of evil. We become captive to the spirit of the age.

And you He made alive, who were dead in trespasses and sins, in which you once walked according to the course of this world, according to the prince of the power of the air, the spirit who now works in the sons of disobedience, among whom also we all once conducted ourselves in the lusts of our flesh, fulfilling the desires of the flesh and of the mind, and were by nature children of wrath, just as the others (Ephesians 2:1-3).

A good example of this is what is in style or fashion. Have you ever noticed how when fashion changes you may at first be reluctant, but in the end you find yourself going along? One day my mother was wearing a lime green blouse. It was a color from the 70's and I hated the 70's styles. I was a teenager then, but looking back I remember shag carpets, paisley shirts, and bellbottoms. By the time you read this book they may well be in style again or be one of those styles from yesteryear. I commented on my mom's ugly blouse and laughed at her willingness to buy something ugly just because it was in style. My surprise was that one day I was in a store and they had a black tie with that same green, and I found myself thinking "wow that really does look good!" Whatever the fashion, whether in clothes or house décor, sooner or later everybody goes along until somewhere somebody comes up with something else and the cycle begins all over again. My experience seems to indicate about every thirty years.

Those who live outside God's kingdom have sold themselves to another power. They walk under the influence of others without even knowing it. The point is sooner or later we give in to the influences around us unless we maintain a vigilant stand that governs our choices. This is also true about the spirit of the age.

Note the scripture in Ephesians talks not only about the disobedient but those who live for desires of our flesh, our mind and our human nature. One of the greatest fallacies about the devil is he is trying to get you to serve him. His greatest tool against us is not to get us to serve him but to get us to serve ourselves. When we choose to serve ourselves the devil becomes our master and we don't even know what is happening to us. It is like the peanuts cartoon I saw once. Linus says; "we have found the enemy and it is us!" Self-centeredness is the great enemy of man and the church. It is self-centeredness that destroys families, churches, and yes, even countries. This is why we must observe the power of the dragon and make our choice to defeat him.

Before we discuss in detail the dragon and beasts we need to understand fully the concept of Babylon. We know that Babylon was a literal place, a people who were the enemies of God's people and the ones who held them captive when the judgment of God came upon them. Although Babylon became the enemy of God's people, she was still just a tool for the purposes of God.

> *Be in pain, and labor to bring forth, O daughter of Zion, Like a woman in birth pangs. For now you shall go forth from the city, You shall dwell in the field, And to Babylon you shall go. There you shall be delivered; There the LORD will redeem you From the hand of your enemies* (Micah 4:10).

When God was done with Babylon He judged them for what they have done to His people to demonstrate His power and sovereignty in all things.

> *Then he cried, "A lion, my Lord! I stand continually on the watchtower in the daytime; I have sat at my post every night. And look, here comes a chariot of men with a pair of horsemen!" Then he answered and said, "Babylon is fallen, is*

fallen! And all the carved images of her gods He has broken to the ground" (Isaiah 21:8-9).

The concept of Babylon needs to be fully explored in order for us to understand what the source of her power is. The root for Babylon is "Babel" whose story is told in the book of Genesis chapter 11. In the story of Babel mankind decided he would "make a name for himself" and build a tower to heaven. This tower was built with bricks. This innovation replaced the stones God had made with bricks made through the power of human effort and ingenuity. This power demonstrates rebellion against God and a desire to make something for oneself rather than to trust in God. It is a story no different than the one in the garden. The idea is independence from God will bring freedom. God instead sent confusion to the nations. Isaiah, the prophet, spoke of God's judgment against Babylon in Isaiah 14. Babylon here represents rebellion against God personified.

"How you are fallen from heaven, O Lucifer, son of the morning! How you are cut down to the ground, You who weakened the nations! For you have said in your heart: 'I will ascend into heaven, I will exalt my throne above the stars of God; I will also sit on the mount of the congregation On the farthest sides of the north...'" (Isaiah 14:12-13).

We see in this Scripture the word Lucifer used. The original word (heylel) is better translated as "morning star." The translation as Lucifer used in some texts gives the bias of the translators by inferring that the devil is a fallen angel called Lucifer. We must again avoid private interpretations of Scripture but let the Bible interpret itself. The term morning star is actually given to Jesus Christ in Revelation 22:16 and is promised to the overcoming Christian in Revelation 2:28. The term morning star actually refers to the planet Venus that is seen on the horizon before the dawning of a new day. It refers to the first sign of hope or light, which makes it an appropriate name for Jesus Christ and His church but certainly should not be used to speak of satan. Many leaders start out offering hope for the future but in the end the hope becomes another empty dream! This is a prophecy against Babylon as clearly stated in verse four. The attitude of "ascending to the heavens" falls under the same attitude as at the tower of Babel. It certainly reflects the attitude of the most well known King of Babylon, Nebuchadnezzer. His pride lifted the king to a place of self-exaltation that set him against God.

> *At the end of the twelve months he was walking about the royal palace of Babylon. The king spoke, saying, "Is not this great Babylon, that I have built for a royal dwelling by my mighty power and for the honor of my majesty?" While the word was still in the king's mouth, a voice fell from heaven: "King Nebuchadnezzar, to you it is spoken: the kingdom has departed from you!"* (Daniel 4:29-31)

Nebuchadnezzer not only exalted himself in his pride but he had also built a god of his own and forced the people to worship it. How much more could one be in rebellion and self-exaltation than to make your own god? In the book of Daniel chapter eight when speaking of political powers exalting themselves it uses the imagery of stars and the prince of the host.

> *And out of one of them came a little horn which grew exceedingly great toward the south, toward the east, and toward the Glorious Land. And it grew up to the host of heaven; and it cast down some of the host and some of the stars to the ground, and trampled them. He even exalted himself as high as the Prince of the host; and by him the daily sacrifices were taken away, and the place of His sanctuary was cast down* (Daniel 8:9-11).

It is very important to understand in prophetic imagery the stories of humanity are seen in the great spiritual realm that overshadows them. Yet, in the end both the sin and the judgment come in the natural.

> *"For I will rise up against them," says the LORD of hosts, "And cut off from Babylon the name and remnant, And offspring and posterity," says the LORD. "I will also make it a possession for the porcupine, And marshes of muddy water; I will sweep it with the broom of destruction," says the LORD of hosts* (Isaiah 14:22-23).

The final moral of the story is that God is God all the time and no rebellion or effort outside His will shall prevail in the end. Yet there is always a realm outside His perfect place for us that He will allow us to choose if we want to. The judgment and pain of this choice is not just for our punishment but it is for our training. God's love and hope is always for us, waiting for us to return to Him when we are ready. When we come to Him He will in no way cast us out!

It is time to recognize God's judgment is upon Babylon. God's judgment is upon all human effort outside the will and purpose of God. We who see ourselves in the Kingdom of God need to recognize we can't be in the Kingdom of God and Babylon at the same time. It is time to come out of Babylon and fully embrace our citizenship in the Kingdom of God.

> *And he cried mightily with a loud voice, saying, "Babylon the great is fallen, is fallen, and has become a dwelling place of demons, a prison for every foul spirit, and a cage for every unclean and hated bird! For all the nations have drunk of the wine of the wrath of her fornication, the kings of the earth have committed fornication with her, and the merchants of the earth have become rich through the abundance of her luxury." And I heard another voice from heaven saying, "Come out of her, my people, lest you share in her sins, and lest you receive of her plagues"* (Revelation 18:2-4).

The devil and his messengers inhabit the realms of Babylon. If we do not separate ourselves we will be bound to her actions and power. God wants us in His Kingdom demonstrating His power.

Chapter Six

THE BEAST AND THE DRAGON

Revelation 12 is an allegorical picture showing us the triumph of Christ at the time of His resurrection. When He ascends into heaven there is a war between a dragon and Michael, the archangel, who was the protector and guardian of the children of God. Michael prevails in the conflict and the dragon is cast down to the earth. This dragon John tells us is actually the serpent of old, called the devil and satan. After this heavenly conflict this dragon goes to earth to make war with the woman, the bride of Christ, and her offspring, those who have the testimony of Jesus Christ and are the sons of God. The sons of God will overcome the enemy by the blood of the Lamb, the word of their testimony, and their willingness to give up their lives for the cause of Christ. It is essential we understand the devil knows his time is limited and that the day of his demise will come at the hands of the seed of the women. This fulfills the prophecy given in the book of Genesis chapter 3 and demonstrates the Word of God will always come to pass. The purposes of God will not be withheld from Him! Having discussed all of this in the previous chapters, we can move into the understanding of the conflict as demonstrated in Revelation chapter 13.

John sees a beast coming out of the sea. This beast has seven heads and ten horns an exact description of the dragon mentioned in chapter 12. The Scriptures tell us the dragon gives his authority and power to the beast. It is obvious this is simply another personification of the dragon. We read that on the beasts head was a "blasphemous" name and that he speaks blasphemy. Blasphemy means to speak evil against someone. Like the devil, the accuser of the brethren, his speaking forth and his words are deadly. This beast also speaks blasphemous things railing against God and His people. This beast has authority over the nations similar to the god of this world, satan, who has blinded the eyes of this world and holds it captive to his devices. It is important to note the people worship the beast and also the dragon that gives it power. They do not necessarily know it is the dragon because the deception is in what the dragon offers, a beast that mesmerizes them.

It is important as we observe the prophecy of John for us to consider the fact that what he says follows the pattern of the prophets of the Old Testament. When receiving these visions I am sure John had specific things in mind, as did the prophets of the Old Testament who spoke of God's impending judgment upon the adversaries of Israel. I am sure John saw Rome as fulfilling many of the attributes of the beast systems. Like Daniel of the Old Testament, he certainly would have seen this beast as representing kings and kingdoms that so often are the enemy of the purposes and people of God. Rome certainly had a hand in the crucifixion of Jesus Christ and also the persecution of the Christian church in its early history. However, we need to understand the dragon is the real power behind the thrones of men. Ultimately the system or political power is not the real problem but simply represents the deeper spiritual problem underlying the system. The powers of the dragon and hence the systems are ultimately the result of the wrong attitudes and actions of people. The beast or dragon is not the problem as much as the heart attitudes and carnal thinking that give it authority in our lives. The dragon gets its power the same way the serpent did and will be defeated the same way. Our warfare still involves tearing down the strongholds of thinking and attitudes that exalt themselves against the knowledge of God as well as bringing our minds into the captivity of obedience to Christ.

It is important at this juncture to also remember the dragon and the beast are of no threat to God and His ultimate purpose. Throughout history God has used the evil intent of man to fulfill His purpose and in the end will judge the system when He brings healing and restoration to His people. This was the example of Babylon in the Old Testament. First God uses it as an instrument of His judgment.

> For thus says the LORD: "Behold, I will make you a terror to yourself and to all your friends; and they shall fall by the sword of their enemies, and your eyes shall see it. I will give all Judah into the hand of the king of Babylon, and he shall carry them captive to Babylon and slay them with the sword. Moreover I will deliver all the wealth of this city, all its produce, and all its precious things; all the treasures of the kings of Judah I will give into the hand of their enemies, who will plunder them, seize them, and carry them to Babylon" (Jeremiah 20:4-5).

After God is done He uses the instrument of his judgment so He can punish the wickedness of the enemy and restore His people.

> "'Then it will come to pass, when seventy years are completed, that I will punish the king of Babylon and that nation, the land of the Chaldeans, for their iniquity,' says the LORD; 'and I will make it a perpetual desolation. So I will bring on that land all My words which I have pronounced against it, all that is written in this book, which Jeremiah has prophesied concerning all the nations. (For many nations and great kings shall be served by them also; and I will repay them according to their deeds and according to the works of their own hands.)'" (Jeremiah 25:12-14).

Oh the wisdom and the justice of God! Unfortunately, because we do not see the power and the sovereignty of our God we often spend our time trying to figure out who the enemy is rather than getting ourselves in right standing with God. Our battle is for the hearts and minds of people. This is also the goal of the enemy. The beast of Revelation wants to put his mark on the heads and the hands of the people. He will use the pressure of human need to get people to receive his mark or be influenced by his persuasion. This

69

is in contrast to the people of God whose minds and hearts belong to God. As the dragon, the devil uses human institutions to gain influence over us. We need to understand the way he uses systems so we can fully overcome him. Many times when we see the power of the system we are drawn into conflict with the system causing us to lose our spiritual power over it.

An example of this is when the beast or system is political in nature. In the United States there was a definite turn in the wrong direction morally as the late 1960's began to unfold. In the early 1970's the Supreme Court ruled abortion controls were an illegal infringement upon the rights of a woman. This led to the over-turning of many more laws about morality in the country un-leashing an onslaught of moral change. The change in moral behavior became very evident with new guidelines in the media allowing all manner of promiscuous behavior to be broadcast over the airwaves. The sense of outrage in the Christian community was palpable and everyone began to look for ways they could turn the tide. The Bible gives us very important insight into our strat-egy in times like this.

> *According to their deeds, accordingly He will repay, Fury to*
> *His adversaries, Recompense to His enemies; The coastlands*
> *He will fully repay. So shall they fear The name of the LORD*
> *from the west, And His glory from the rising of the sun; When*
> *the enemy comes in like a flood, The Spirit of the LORD will*
> *lift up a standard against him (Isaiah 59:18-19).*

Of course, our strategy begins with a turning to God as our source understanding in the end He will always judge unrighteous-ness. In Revelation chapter 12 the enemy sends a flood against the woman and the earth opens up its mouth to swallow it up and pro-tect her. We need to know God is always aware of us and will deliver us in the appointed time. God wants to raise up a standard against the enemy and the standard must come from the house of God. The issue isn't really what is happening in the world but what is happening in the church. Our strength and power is within not without. When the church understands who we are and what is inside of us we will never be intimidated by the world.

> *You are of God, little children, and have overcome them, because He who is in you is greater than he who is in the world. They are of the world. Therefore they speak as of the world, and the world hears them. We are of God. He who knows God hears us; he who is not of God does not hear us. By this we know the spirit of truth and the spirit of error* (1 John 4:4-6).

Sinners sin! Why does it surprise us when people live according to who they are? The issue isn't how bad the world is but is the church salt and light in the midst of it.

> *"You are the salt of the earth; but if the salt loses its flavor, how shall it be seasoned? It is then good for nothing but to be thrown out and trampled underfoot by men." "You are the light of the world. A city that is set on a hill cannot be hidden. Nor do they light a lamp and put it under a basket, but on a lampstand, and it gives light to all who are in the house. Let your light so shine before men, that they may see your good works and glorify your Father in heaven"* (Matthew 5:13-16).

The glory of God is revealed through the church. When we stand in contrast to the world God receives the glory by our testimony. It has always been God's desire to have a people out of a people. When God gets what He wants then He will pour out His blessing to us and we will be a source of blessing to the world. This is the promise God made to Abraham and is still the promise and plan of God for our day.

> *"I will make you a great nation; I will bless you And make your name great; And you shall be a blessing. I will bless those who bless you, And I will curse him who curses you; And in you all the families of the earth shall be blessed"* (Genesis 12:2-3).

71

In 1980 I attended a meeting in Dallas, Texas at the behest of one of my members where the ministers were encouraged to join the political system. We were told the answer to our moral dilemma was in our involvement with the political system. This message was met with rounding applause from the crowd of several thousand and a new political movement ensued. After thirty years of involvement the results have been negligible. As a Christian in a democratic society, I believe it is an issue of stewardship to be informed and involved. If you have a responsibility it should be seen as a stewardship from God and should be handled with a clear mandate of this responsibility. However, the error comes when the church joins the system and as Christians fail to see our weapons of war are not carnal but spiritual. At this point we fail to be the influence we are called of God to be. The spiritual vitality of the Christian church in America has declined with our involvement as a part of the system rather than as ambassadors for the Kingdom of God.

This is where the understanding of the sons of God and the bride of Christ come to the forefront. Revelation 12 talks about the woman, the bride of Christ, and her offspring, which represents the sons of God as individuals before God. The bride should never join herself to any system of man. The bride's allegiance and loyalty belongs only to her husband. This is why the Lord admonished the Old Testament bride not to call for a confederacy with other nations but to put her trust in God.

> *"Do not say, 'A conspiracy,' Concerning all that this people call a conspiracy, Nor be afraid of their threats, nor be troubled. The LORD of hosts, Him you shall hallow; Let Him be your fear, And let Him be your dread. He will be as a sanctuary, But a stone of stumbling and a rock of offense To both the houses of Israel, As a trap and a snare to the inhabitants of Jerusalem"* (Isaiah 8:12-14).

The word conspiracy is translated confederacy in the KJV. Both words help us understand the point, which is not to have an unlawful alliance because we are afraid of the power of the enemies we face. Now as individuals called of God, we may be called to politics, entertainment, the media, or any other realm but this must be fully distinguished from the woman, or bride of God, who dwells in the wilderness prepared for her by God and who finds her protection and help solely in Him. This is why religious freedom is important for the benefit of the church, but alliances and support from outside sources will become traps that will in the end lead to judgment.

History has bore this out. European nations have often mixed government and religion. Many of the churches in Europe have been supported and financed by the government. The end result of this system has been churches who often become oppressors of the people for the purpose of political power. They have often been pawns in the hand of government in exchange for their support of the policies of the government. When the United States was founded religion was very important and often encouraged by the leaders, but there was a strong line between church and state so the integrity of religious freedom could be maintained. In this environment the American church not only prospered but also became a force of evangelism throughout the world. If we as Christians believe our beliefs to be superior those beliefs will certainly be able to compete in an open structure without special benefits from government.

When I was a kid I loved history and current events. Since I became a Christian as a young person, I also observed these things from a Christian perspective. I remember thinking at the end of World War II how sad it must have been for Eastern Europe to come under the sway of the Soviet Union. This system was anti-religion so the thought was how sad for the church in these countries. Western Europe on the other hand was free so the church could continue to operate with freedom. Interesting enough after the end of the cold war and the breakdown of the iron curtain we see that the eastern side of Europe is more spiritually vibrant than the west where less then 3% of the people attend church and most of the grand cathedrals serve more as museums of the past than centers of great spiritual influence. Many of the Western European nations not only had this freedom but many times had the implicit support of the governments to boot. In the end these supports became a substitute for reliance upon God and became a hindrance rather than a help to the purposes of God.

This picture is amply demonstrated in the whore of Babylon John saw in his revelation. This woman was not the beast but sat upon the beast. She was a harlot for she found her sustenance in the beast that was not her husband but her lover. This woman receives her strength from the kings and merchants of the earth. She is in stark contrast to the bride of Christ who inhabits the wilderness, a place prepared for her by the Lord. The harlot even is drunk from the blood of the martyrs. In the end the harlot's judgment comes from her lovers. The Lord puts it into their hearts to hate her and make her desolate. Again, I am sure John saw this caricature as part of the influence of Rome for the beast had seven heads representing the seven hills the city of Rome was on and this city ruled the nations of the world. But we must also be aware that part of the power of Rome was to use religion as a way to control people. Early Christians were considered as atheists by Roman authorities because they only believed in one God rather than the pantheon of gods Rome extolled. We must see the caricatures of the Revelation as being systems represented by many different philosophies over history but with the same principles guiding them. Many Protestants saw the whore of Babylon as the Roman Church. This could certainly be true in certain times of history but it could also be true of Protestant churches. When we see the subtle deceptions of the enemy we can see how all churches and people can come under the sway of the dragon if we are not careful. This is why we should not label them specifically but should consider the spirit they represent!

When you survey history from this perspective you can see how God has dealt with the church just as He did with Israel. When they would sin God would allow them to come under the influences of powers that would judge them. When they would repent God would deliver them and let His power work for them. I see this pattern in Russian history. The Russian church in time became a supported system by the government of Russian. The church was wedded to the government. When communism came to power they turned on the church and the church came under great tribulation. It is interesting to me the power of the Soviet system lasted about 70 years the same as the duration of the judgment of Israel under the rule of Babylon. Unfortunately, the Russian Orthodox Church has in many ways fallen back into their old ways. Rather than promote freedom of religion many are trying to use the influence of government and its sister "nationalism" to gain the Orthodox Church special favors from the government. This is why a political solution can be so disastrous for the church. In this situation, we begin to feel the government is our source and supply and we forget God is the source and supply that will never run dry. Again, competition becomes the life of a church vitally connected to God. When the church is connected to government it will seek a favorable environment for its activities and will even seek to persecute those who are against it.

This is the pattern of Christian church history. When John received his revelation the church was under severe persecution. He was an exile on the Isle of Patmos when the Lord came to him. Although the Roman Empire was an enemy at the time, in a few hundred years a Roman Emperor by the name of Constantine would be born again and make Christianity the religion of the Roman Empire. The church flourished for a while but in time became married to the system. Eventually, the persecuted church became the persecuting church and those who stood against the Church of Rome became victims of her power. This is the picture many Protestants have when claiming the Roman Church to be the whore of Babylon, but it wasn't long before even the protestant reformers fell into the same mode. Even John Calvin, the great reformer, was guilty of this crime when his theology prevailed in Geneva, Switzerland. It is so easy to fall under the deception of the dragon or devil and think at the same time you are doing God a favor. The Bible talks about the works of the flesh and the fruit of the spirit. It is very easy to judge the difference when the Word of God prevails. When the devil is at work he can blind our eyes. Murders, hatred, strife, animosity are always the work of the flesh. In modern America some religious zealots have considered themselves the sword of God by killing abortionists. Jesus was certainly right when He said; "if you live by the sword you will die by the sword."

In this discussion the root sin where the enemy gains his stronghold is the pride of life. Pride motivates us to build confidence in ourselves and the system of ideas we believe in. It is also the root for nationalism and ethnic pride that motivates people to find their identity and confidence in the things of this world. This pride motivation was the source of inspiration for Nazism or National Socialism, which led to the horrible killing machine that exterminated millions of Jews and caused unknown numbers of deaths. This pride in the superiority of ideals motivated the communists of the Soviet Union and China to kill tens of millions of people. How well the Bible says it when it says, "there is a way that seems right to a man but its end is the way of death!"

As Christians our citizenship allegiance must first be in heaven. Rather than seek for pride in our human identity we should seek to glory in the Lord.

> But "he who glories, let him glory in the LORD." For not he who commends himself is approved, but whom the Lord commends (2 Corinthians 10:17-18).

As a Christian I must see myself from a kingdom perspective first and foremost. When I do this I will not perform the works of the flesh but will manifest the fruit of the Spirit as Jesus Christ did when he walked on the earth. . It is time for the church to take her place with Christ sitting in heavenly places with a heavenly perspective.

> And God raised us up with Christ and seated us with him in the heavenly realms in Christ Jesus, in order that in the coming ages he might show the incomparable riches of his grace, expressed in his kindness to us in Christ Jesus (Ephesians 2:6-7 NIV).

Chapter Seven

THE POWER OF DARKNESS

When man faced the choice of obedience to God or death he chose death. This was not immediate physical death but spiritual death. This spiritual death led to physical death as a result of being cut off from the life of God. Many times when people sin it seems like they are "getting away with it." This is because sin has a payday but it is not always immediate. We have mentioned how the devil offers us shortcuts in life. These short cuts often lead us to a long road of death and alienation from God.

> *There is a way that seems right to a man, But its end is the way of death* (Proverbs 16:2).

Our shortsighted thinking is, unfortunately, the devil's door to our heart. The death God told Adam about was actually enslavement. This enslavement would take us from the realm of freedom of choice, which was what God offered, to the bondage of slavery, which is what the devil's advice brought to us.

> *And you He made alive, who were dead in trespasses and sins, in which you once walked according to the course of this world, according to the prince of the power of the air, the **spirit who now works in the sons of disobedience,** among whom also we all once conducted ourselves in the lusts of our flesh, fulfilling the desires of the flesh and of the mind, and were by nature children of wrath, just as the others* (Ephesians 2:1-3).

When we are spiritually dead we don't even realize we are a slave to the world and our base instincts. We, in our pride, often think very highly of ourselves and yet we are sold to this lie of the enemy. God created us as spiritual beings motivated by the high level of spiritual discernment that only God can give. Our human spirit is the breath of God that gives us the greatest level of understanding.

> *But there is a spirit in man, And the breath of the Almighty gives him understanding. Great men are not always wise, Nor do the aged always understand justice* (Job 32:8-9).

This is the deception of our modern era. In our so-called wisdom, man has decided the world was not created but simply appeared. Out of nothing came something that eventually through "natural selection" produced the world we live in. This theory of evolution makes us worship the creation rather than the creator.

> *Professing to be wise, they became fools, and changed the glory of the incorruptible God into an image made like corruptible man—and birds and four-footed animals and creeping things. Therefore God also gave them up to uncleanness, in the lusts of their hearts, to dishonor their bodies among themselves, who exchanged the truth of God for the lie, and worshiped and served the creature rather than the Creator, who is blessed forever. Amen* (Romans 1:22-25).

As I mentioned earlier, I believe responsible stewardship will make us conscious of our need to respectfully care for our natural resources. However, the secular world has taken this a step further and has made us in many ways subservient to the natural order. This is the spirit of the world that declares mankind is what has destroyed the planet. They will maintain that the natural world would be better without us. It is a scary thought isn't it? But the wisdom of man is always self-destructive in the end. The enemy has turned us against ourselves and we don't even know it. This is in fact divine judgment. We now worship the creation and in the end we become the slave. The result of this judgment is we now consider man to be just an intelligent animal.

The result of this is animal like behaviors that are causing us to deny and invalidate our purpose. How far we have fallen from the place God desires us to be. The word declares in this state of being we will actually live with a nature that is in opposition to the nature God has given to us. This picture is very evident in our day.

> *Therefore God also gave them up to uncleanness, in the lusts of their hearts, to dishonor their bodies among themselves, who exchanged the truth of God for the lie, and worshiped and served the creature rather than the Creator, who is blessed forever. Amen. For this reason God gave them up to vile passions. For even their women exchanged the natural use for what is against nature. Likewise also the men, leaving the natural use of the woman, burned in their lust for one another, men with men committing what is shameful, and receiving in themselves the penalty of their error which was due. And even as they did not like to retain God in their knowledge, God gave them over to a debased mind, to do those things which are not fitting; being filled with all unrighteousness, sexual immorality, wickedness, covetousness, maliciousness; full of envy, murder, strife, deceit, evil-mindedness; they are whisperers, backbiters, haters of God, violent, proud, boasters, inventors of evil things, disobedient to parents, undiscerning, untrustworthy, unloving, unforgiving, unmerciful; who, knowing the righteous judgment of God, that those who practice such things are deserving of death, not only do the same but also approve of those who practice them* (Romans 1:24-32).

Today, the rise of sexual immorality is an obvious example. People not only act immorally they expect and unfortunately receive the approval of our greater society. If you will notice accompanying this is also an increase of violence, anger, breakdowns in relationships, and hardness of heart. What an angry and unmerciful world we live in. But please note, there comes a point where these behaviors are not a choice but a curse inflicted upon the people. God gives people over to what they choose, but in the end they become sold to the bondage of their choice. People give themselves over to the power of the enemy. In this way the devil becomes the Lord's jailer. He is allowed to fill the void created by the disobedience of man. Remember darkness is the absence of light. We open the door and darkness comes billowing in. The prince of the power of the air takes advantage of our disobedience and then begins to sell us more and more into his persuasions. What a sad end for those God created for His purpose, for those created to share His glory. God created us as unique in the creation. He created us in His image to be His sons and walk in dominion. God's plan of redemption will not only give us eternal life but will also bring us out of the slavery of sin and the power of the devil bringing us to our rightful position. He will lead us to the place He has called us to from the beginning.

This is the picture of the salvation God has chosen for us!

> . . . *giving thanks to the Father who has qualified us to be partakers of the inheritance of the saints in the light. He has delivered us from the power of darkness and conveyed us into the kingdom of the Son of His love, in whom we have redemption through His blood, the forgiveness of sins* (Colossians 1:12-14).

When we become a Christian we are literally translated from the power of darkness to the Kingdom of God. The word power here means authority. When we are alienated from God we come under the authority or power of the devil. In this condition we are considered dead and really a slave to the enemy. The devil has authority over us when we leave the Father's kingdom. The devil reigns in the realm of darkness and feasts on our "dust" or fleshly motivations. When we turn to Jesus Christ as our Savior we experience a profound spiritual change. God chooses us and then He gives us the gift of choice. Now we are responsible for the choices we make.

Once we see how this process works we must be very careful to keep ourselves from the place of bondage that comes from walking out of the light of God into the darkness of the age. This is how the Apostle John saw what I am describing.

> **Blessed are those who do His commandments,** *that they may have* **the right to the tree of life,** *and may enter through the gates into the city.* **But outside** *are dogs and sorcerers and sexually immoral and murderers and idolaters, and whoever loves and practices a lie* (Revelation 22:14-15).

The picture here is the picture of our world. Our world is comprised of two parts. We have God's city, or the Kingdom of God established by Jesus Christ when He came, and we have outside the realm of His kingdom, operating by the prevailing power of the devil. As it was in the beginning, when we walk in the Kingdom of God we have access to the Tree of Life, Jesus Christ, and have eternal life abiding in us. When you live outside the city you are outside the life of God. The psalmist spoke of the glories of the marvelous City of God we enter when we are born again.

> *There is a river whose streams shall make glad the city of God, The holy place of the tabernacle of the Most High. God is in the midst of her, she shall not be moved; God shall help her, just at the break of dawn* (Psalm 46:4-5).

> **Glorious things are spoken of you, O city of God!** *And of Zion it will be said, "This one and that one were born in her; And the Most High Himself shall establish her." The LORD will record,* **When He registers the peoples: "This one was born there"** (Psalm 87:3-6).

When Jesus Christ came to the earth He came to announce the reign of the Kingdom of God. He also spoke of the fact that in order for the earth to be overwhelmed by the message and power of the Kingdom of God He had to engage in a serious confrontation with the god of this world, satan. He said: "in order for you to

81

take the strongman's house you must first bind the strongman then you can take the goods of his house." The confrontation with the strongman would result in the stripping of his authority and give empowerment to the church to do the clean up job of repossessing his territory. This confrontation with the strongman certainly gives us an important visual of the role and rule of satan. This confrontation would also involve the direct confrontation with the devil's messengers, also called devils or demons. The demonstration of Jesus' power over the demonic realm was a sign of His authority. When Jesus was casting out demons the people said He was casting out demons by the power of Beelzebub. Jesus brought the conversation to a discussion of the Kingdom of God and the power of the devil.

> *If Satan also is divided against himself, how will his kingdom stand? Because you say I cast out demons by Beelzebub. And if I cast out demons by Beelzebub, by whom do your sons cast them out? Therefore they will be your judges. But if I cast out demons with the finger of God, surely the kingdom of God has come upon you* (Luke 11:18-20).

There are two realms on the earth, the kingdom governed by God and the realm governed by the devil. These kingdoms cannot overlap from the point of view of Jesus Christ. When a person is born again they are translated from one realm to the other. The new birth involves a deliverance from evil.

> *He has delivered us from the power of darkness and conveyed us into the kingdom of the Son of His love* . . . (Colossians 1:13).

Before we come to Christ we are under the influence of the spirit of the world. This condition makes us dead to God, but when we turn to the Lord we become alive and free from the spirit that works in the children of disobedience.

in which you once walked according to the course of this world, according to the prince of the power of the air, the spirit who now works in the sons of disobedience, among whom also we all once conducted ourselves in the lusts of our flesh, fulfilling the desires of the flesh and of the mind, and were by nature children of wrath, just as the others. But God, who is rich in mercy, because of His great love with which He loved us, even when we were dead in trespasses, made us alive together with Christ (by grace you have been saved), and raised us up together, and made us sit together in the heavenly places in Christ Jesus . . . (Ephesians 2:2-6).

Our experience with Christ spiritually translates us to the heavenly realm. When a person is filled with the Holy Spirit they are sealed until the day of redemption.

In Him you also trusted, after you heard the word of truth, the gospel of your salvation; in whom also, having believed, you were sealed with the Holy Spirit of promise . . . (Ephesians 1:13).

The word sealed here means, to set a seal or signet upon something for security or preservation. You are separated from the devil's realm and preserved for the power of God. The devil does not have power over you. Anything the devil does concerning you must pass the permission process of God. This is why a believer cannot be possessed by a devil. Many Christians sincerely trying to help others who are under the influence of fleshly temptations have sought to deliver people from their desires by exorcism. The works of the flesh are the works of the flesh not the works of demons. The works of the flesh are clearly listed in the book of Galatians chapter 5 and no matter how compelling these urges are they should not be attributed to the works of the realm of the demonic.

Where does the ministry of the "casting out of demons" come in? If you will notice the Scripture that addresses the casting out of demons reports Jesus saying this:

> *"But if I cast out demons with the finger of God, surely the kingdom of God has come upon you"* (Luke 11:20).

This ministry is obviously the finger of God reaching into the realm of darkness. In every case of demon possession brought to Jesus Christ the person was in an out of control state. The person was tormented and in such darkness that someone else brought them to receive the help they needed. When a demon possessed person is delivered it brings them to the place of freedom of choice where they can choose the way of God or not. Although we can assume many of the people were part of the Jewish religion, this was not able to protect them or deliver them because they were not truly in a heartfelt covenant with God. Jesus was very adamant that religion passed on through the generations would not put us in right standing with God. We must have a true heartfelt conversion. Once we have freedom of choice then we must choose to follow the ways of God and walk in the light of the Kingdom of God or our end state will be worse than our first.

When we understand the importance of choice we see how a person can give in to demonic influence through their choices. Yet, when thinking about demonic influences Christians should not take the view they are protected from the demonic realm simply through their new birth experience. As we have learned the power of the devil in the beginning came from disobedience. Like Adam and Eve before us, we can give him authority in our lives when we fail to live according to the standard God has given to us. The devil feeds on flesh and when we live in the flesh we give him and his helpers room in our lives. Our goal must be to not give him room.

Jesus spoke of this when speaking about demons and deliverance:

> *"When an unclean spirit goes out of a man, he goes through dry places, seeking rest; and finding none, he says, 'I will return to my house from which I came.' And when he comes, he finds it swept and put in order. Then he goes and takes with him seven other spirits more wicked than himself, and they*

enter and dwell there; and the last state of that man is worse than the first" (Luke 11:24-26).

I remember when I was a young man; I went to a church that was teaching deliverance ministry through casting demons out of people. Afterward they would tell the people, "you now need to fill the room with the Holy Spirit so the demon can't come back." We would see people prayed over for deliverance and get them speaking in tongues and rejoicing at their great deliverance. Unfortunately, this process would be repeated on a weekly basis and most people just kept going through the ritual until they became discouraged and gave up. The back door of the church was constantly swinging. People were coming in and going out and we didn't realize the problem was not the students but the teachers. Rather than telling people to get more filled with God so the devil wouldn't have room to come in we should have been telling them to get rid of the room. The room is the place in our actions or thinking that makes a place for the devil. This instruction may seem too simple but looking to the Word it says just don't make a place for the devil.

"Be angry, and do not sin": do not let the sun go down on your wrath, nor give place to the devil (Ephesians 4:26-27).

These Scriptures show how this principle works. Anger is a work of the flesh. Anger comes very easy and is not in itself a sin. Unresolved anger, however, does provide room for the devil and can certainly lead to sin. If we become angry and deal with it we will be okay. We deal with it by just calming ourselves, seeking the peace of God, or finding the right path for our anger. Sometimes this can be done through dealing with the situation or if it involves people talking through the problem. Don't wait too long or your anger can grow and other works of the flesh can manifest such as: strife, resentment, envy, jealousy, etc. The Bible also says that people who do not choose the road of peace can develop a root of bitterness that defiles themselves and those around them. Whatever the end result, we have made a room for the demonic realm and can easily sell ourselves into bondage.

Many people will come to the Lord and experience a great deliverance from the bondage of sin. We must be very careful to get rid of rooms or places in our lives and hearts the devil can come into. Don't just clean up your act. Get rid of the room! Repentance and self-examination should be a regular part of our Christian walk. This is why communion is so vital. At the Lord's Table we should judge ourselves regularly so we are not judged and condemned with the world. When we maintain this attitude we are always getting rid of rooms that can cause trouble. In our humility, we are also acknowledging our culpability in the bondages of our lives. In the garden when God confronted Adam he pointed a finger at Eve, Eve pointed her finger at the serpent and, of course, he didn't have a leg to stand on! Accepting the responsibility for our choices and actions will defeat the devil every time.

This shows us how important it is to keep our focus. We must keep ourselves for the Lord by walking in the light of His word at all times. By walking in the light of the Lord we keep ourselves filled with light.

> *"The lamp of the body is the eye. Therefore, when your eye is good, your whole body also is full of light. But when your eye is bad, your body also is full of darkness. Therefore take heed that the light which is in you is not darkness. If then your whole body is full of light, having no part dark, the whole body will be full of light, as when the bright shining of a lamp gives you light"* (Luke 11:34-36).

Remember the story of Peter being tested by the devil? Jesus said to Simon Peter, "Satan has asked for you to sift you like wheat, but I have prayed for you and when you return to Me strengthen the brethren." Peter was a brash and self-confident person always stepping to the front of the line to express his opinions and to show his confidence in himself. He knew if confronted with trouble as a disciple, Jesus could have complete confidence in him. It was this confidence that opened the door for the devil and made him a prime candidate for trouble. Jesus knew Peter would fall in the process even to the point of denying him. Yet Jesus prayed for him. He didn't pray that Peter would not face the conflict but that he would be strengthened in it. Peter's problem was not the devil but what gave the devil room in his life. When Peter came to the end of himself and returned to Jesus, he actually came back a better person than before he was tested. Although we should always strive to stay inside the ark of safety this is not always possible. Because of God's grace and mercy all things work together for good for those who love God and are called according to His purpose. We need to always remember the problem is not on the outside but on the inside. For Peter the devil's sifting actually made him into a better person and qualified him to take a leadership role in the church.

Satan is not just a jailer for the guilty but a trainer and equipper when used by the hand of God. It is very important in this story to note satan desired to sift Peter, but he had to have permission. Sometimes that permission comes from us by our lack of spiritual discipline and sometimes it comes from God in order to **develop** our spiritual discipline! Truly God is the God of all things and He is always mindful of His people.

The story of Job aptly demonstrates this principle. Job was a righteous man so much so God is bragging on him to satan in the opening of the book of Job. Satan, as the adversary of man, accuses Job of simply doing what he needs to do because God has been so generous to him. This is why he is also called the devil or accuser of the brethren. Most of us know the story of Job very well. We know of the great suffering and the great patience of Job. In the end, God declares Job really knew Him and spoke about Him in truth not like his so called friends. Now, Job never really understood the full aspects of the story as we know them. This is like our walk today. Many times we cannot fully understand our circumstances or the warfare ensuing around us because we are in the midst of it, but we can know our God. We must always understand in the end our God will work on our behalf and He is "the rewarder of those who diligently seek Him." Like Job, we must have the confidence that God is aware of our circumstance and in the end will demonstrate His glory in and through us. In the end Job received a double portion blessing, and it is this blessing God has in store for us as we fully serve Him.

I believe the other aspect of this story is especially relevant to us today. It is a story that showcases the heavenly realm. The book of Ephesians connects the heavenly realm to the eternal purpose of God.

> *. . . and to make all see what is the fellowship of the mystery, which from the beginning of the ages has been hidden in God who created all things through Jesus Christ; to the intent that now the manifold wisdom of God might be made known by the church to the principalities and powers in the heavenly places, according to the eternal purpose which He accomplished in Christ Jesus our Lord . . .* (Ephesians 3:9-11).

These Scriptures tell us the earth is literally a theatre with a heavenly audience. This audience consists of the spiritual realm where they are witnessing the power, wisdom and glory of the church in this hour. This is why we cannot always be directly involved in the conflict because it is meant to reveal the wisdom of God not the wisdom of men. What we can do is be a demonstration of a person who has faith and confidence in God and display our knowledge that in the end His wisdom will bring our redemption.

The Scriptures say, "Had the rulers of this world known they would not have crucified the Lord of glory." Who would have thought crucifying Jesus was God's way of nailing the devil to the cross and actually defeating him? When we operate in the carnal mind we often miss the plans and purposes of God. It was true in the time of Jesus Christ and it is true in this day. The carnally minded tried to get Jesus to turn from His course. Peter even took up a sword to fight off the soldiers and protect Jesus. He felt so spiritual fighting for Jesus when in fact he was fighting against Him. This is so often true in our lives and especially true when it comes to spiritual conflicts. We approach our conflicts with carnal understanding, and we try to use "spiritual" tools to accomplish our purpose. We call it spiritual warfare and it is carnal warfare. Where would you have been if you were one of Jesus' disciples? Would you have taken up the sword? Or perhaps you would have taken up the "sword of the spirit" to try and bring everything under control? Could you also be guilty of fighting God when trying to fight the devil? It is so hard for us when things are beyond our understanding and control. Control is what they were looking for in the garden and unfortunately often what we are looking for today. God's kingdom is not the realm of human control but the realm of God's will. Jesus spoke of the devil seeking to get permission to sift Peter. He certainly had to seek God's permission to test Job. Is it possible the devil understands spiritual authority more than we do? We should always understand that when we walk out of God's will we are no longer operating under His authority.

Chapter Eight

The Harlot of Babylon

We have learned that the devil has children just like God has children. We need to know who our Father is! The book of Revelation speaks of the bride of Christ, the Lamb's wife. She is clean, arrayed in fine, white, linen and she must make herself ready for the marriage supper of the Lamb. She dwells in the wilderness in the place that God has prepared for her. He has made a covenant of protection with her and is with her in this place. Her goal is to be the chaste and virtuous woman who is preparing herself for the groom, Christ. The bride of Christ does not speak of one person, but of all the people of God who together are the source of His help and identification in the earth. As seen in Revelation 12, she has been chosen to bear and nurture the seed of Christ and to bring forth the overcoming company with the aid of her husband, Christ. The Word of God calls her the heavenly Jerusalem and the mother of the people of God.

The devil, as one should expect, isn't looking for a chaste bride in whom he can enter into a covenant. Instead, he is joined with a harlot called Babylon. The harlot sits on a scarlet beast. She is not looking for commitment, just the reward of her favors.

So he carried me away in the Spirit into the wilderness. And I saw a woman sitting on a scarlet beast which was full of names of blasphemy, having seven heads and ten horns. The woman was arrayed in purple and scarlet, and adorned with gold and precious stones and pearls, having in her hand a golden cup full of abominations and the filthiness of her for-nication. And on her forehead a name was written:

MYSTERY, BABYLON THE GREAT, THE MOTHER OF HARLOTS AND OF THE ABOMINATIONS OF THE EARTH (Revelation 17:3-5).

Now, we understand the beast is the system the dragon uses for his purpose. This system takes many forms and throughout history has meant many things, but we want to see the harlot who lives in relation to the beast. Whereas the beast gets his power from the dragon, the woman lives off the beast and the people of the earth. Remember, Babylon represents human effort outside the will and purpose of God. Her source is human aspiration, the desire to live independent of God, and the desire to make a name for herself. The prophecies of Revelation are very similar to the ones in Isaiah and Jeremiah that foretell of the future demise of the City of Babylon. This judgment would be complete and would be handed out by the Medes.

"Behold, I will stir up the Medes against them, Who will not regard silver; And as for gold, they will not delight in it. Also their bows will dash the young men to pieces, And they will have no pity on the fruit of the womb; Their eye will not spare children. And Babylon, the glory of kingdoms, The beauty of the Chaldeans' pride, Will be as when God overthrew Sodom and Gomorrah. It will never be inhabited, Nor will it be set-tled from generation to generation; Nor will the Arabian pitch tents there, Nor will the shepherds make their sheepfolds there" (Isaiah 13:17-20).

At the time of John's revelation, the Babylonian prophecy had long been fulfilled. Babylon as a literal force had fallen into the ash heap of history. Yet, John's prophecy clearly echoes the calls of both Isaiah and Jeremiah. This obviously has spiritual implications that transcend the literal and physical world. I am sure many of John's impressions had actual meaning for his time. He says that this harlot is the city that rules over the kings of the earth, so this no doubt refers to Rome. But we must also glean the full spiritual principles involved in this. As in the prophecy of old, the people of God are warned to, "come out of Babylon so you will not be a partaker of her plagues." Babylon has become degenerate.

> *After these things I saw another angel coming down from heaven, having great authority, and the earth was illuminated with his glory. And he cried mightily with a loud voice, saying, "Babylon the great is fallen, is fallen, and has become a dwelling place of demons, a prison for every foul spirit, and a cage for every unclean and hated bird! For all the nations have drunk of the wine of the wrath of her fornication, the kings of the earth have committed fornication with her, and the merchants of the earth have become rich through the abundance of her luxury"* (Revelation 18:1-3).

Again, Rome was the epitome of Babylon, but this harlot lives off the political and business world and they live off of her. The key word to remember is "harlot." What was the sin of the harlot?

> *And another angel followed, saying, "Babylon is fallen, is fallen, that great city, because she has made all nations drink of the wine of the wrath of her fornication"* (Revelation 14:8).

Fornication, in the original context, speaks of sex outside the bonds of matrimony. Chastity in modern times is hard for the average person to comprehend since it has fallen so far in the esteem of modern society. Chastity involves faithfulness and a commitment to the covenant of love. In Scriptures idolatry, or going after false gods, is called adultery or fornication because the people of God are the bride and helper of God just as God ordained the woman as the helper and companion of man. This companionship requiring fidelity and allowing for sexual intimacy is reserved for the man and his wife. The harlot doesn't walk in these principles. Her motivation is the rewards of her labor, her sexuality just being one of her wares for hire. The scarlet of the harlot represents her self-attained wealth and symbolizes her desire to seduce for her purpose. She is a source of evil caused by her provocations.

And on her forehead a name was written:

> MYSTERY, BABYLON THE GREAT, THE MOTHER OF HARLOTS AND OF THE ABOMINATIONS OF THE EARTH (Revelation 17:5).

The word abomination speaks of things that are detestable. Detestable, of course, to God and those committed to His ways. They are certainly not detestable to those who enjoy her pleasures and who have been seduced by her ways.

Babylon as the "devil's woman" becomes his helper and the companion in his pursuits. They are not one in a covenant sense, but their fruit brings the same result. In the Scripture Babylon represents not just a political force, but also a way of life. Remember the story about Daniel and his companions? They were taken to Babylon where the king wanted to conform them to Babylonian ways. Daniel and his companions resisted the ways of Babylon and instead chose to stand on the Word of God and live their lives accordingly. They knew in the end the proof would be manifested as they walked in God's ways instead of walking in the ways of Babylon. The end result was what they had expected and had declared to the people of the court of the king of Babylon.

> So Daniel said to the steward whom the chief of the eunuchs had set over Daniel, Hananiah, Mishael, and Azariah, "Please test your servants for ten days, and let them give us vegetables to eat and water to drink. Then let our appearance be examined before you, and the appearance of the young men who eat the portion of the king's delicacies; and as you see fit, so deal with your servants." So he consented with them in this matter, and tested them ten days. And at the end of ten days their features appeared better and fatter in flesh than all the young men who ate the portion of the king's delicacies (Daniel 1:11-15).

Sanctification is another word that has been neglected by many Christians, and it is robbing the church of its power and ability to witness to the world. Sanctification means to be set apart. Christians are set apart through the blood of the Lamb as the children of God. Once we have been sanctified by God, we must understand the process of sanctification as an on going work in us. This process will make manifest the work of God in us and ultimately demonstrate through us the glory of God. The process of sanctification was initiated through the blood of Jesus Christ, which He willingly gave at Calvary, but continues to work in us as He washes us through His Word.

> *Husbands, love your wives, just as Christ also loved the church and gave Himself for her, that He might sanctify and cleanse her with the washing of water by the word, that He might present her to Himself a glorious church, not having spot or wrinkle or any such thing, but that she should be holy and without blemish* (Ephesians 5:25-27).

Jesus Christ did not die just so you could go to heaven. He died for you so that you would be His bride. He doesn't want just any bride. He wants a glorious bride not having any spots or wrinkles. He told Peter, "I will build my church and the gates of Hades shall not prevail against it." The blessed hope of the church should not just be that Jesus Christ will come and rescue us from this world. Our hope should be that when He comes we will be the people He wants us to be.

> *Beloved, now we are children of God; and it has not yet been revealed what we shall be, but we know that when He is revealed, we shall be like Him, for we shall see Him as He is. And everyone who has this hope in Him purifies himself, just as He is pure* (1 John 3:2-3).

Sanctification is the cleansing we go through as we allow the Word of God to separate us and cleanse us. We experience this process through walking in the Word of Truth.

> *I do not pray that You should take them out of the world, but that You should keep them from the evil one. They are not of the world, just as I am not of the world. Sanctify them by Your truth. Your word is truth. As You sent Me into the world, I also have sent them into the world. And for their sakes I sanctify Myself, that they also may be sanctified by the truth* (John 17:15-19).

Like the people of God who were held captive by Babylon, so it is necessary for us to live in the world that is often against us. We are in the world, but we are not "of" the world. This speaks of our origin. Jesus Christ was not "of" the world because He came from heaven. Like Him, we must understand we are born from above. We must see ourselves as distinct and separate from the world. The devil is the god of this world with a spirit that governs the behavior and patterns of the age. When Jesus Christ was in the wilderness being tested, the devil offered Him the kingdoms of the world if He would simply worship him. The response of Jesus was telling.

> *Then Jesus said to him, "Away with you, Satan! For it is written, 'You shall worship the LORD your God, and Him only you shall serve'"* (Matthew 4:10).

Worship must be connected with service. Many evangelical Christians are selling a false gospel. We are telling people to repeat a formula, and if they will simply say certain words they will be born again and go to heaven. This was not the gospel of the Lord or of His disciples. The message of Jesus was, "Repent for the Kingdom of God is at hand." Jesus Christ and His disciples preached that being born again took a radical departure from their old life, transferring them from the realm of darkness to the realm of light. We are not only called out of darkness into the light, but we are called to be light!

> *. . . for you were once darkness, but now you are light in the Lord. Walk as children of light (for the fruit of the Spirit is in*

all goodness, righteousness, and truth), finding out what is acceptable to the Lord. And have no fellowship with the unfruitful works of darkness, but rather expose them (Ephesians 5:8-11).

Note, you didn't just walk in darkness you were darkness. You were part of the problem. Now you must be part of the answer. We are living in a time when what is detestable in God's eyes is accepted as normal. Many Christians have passively set on the sidelines or been slowly lulled into the thinking and patterns of the world. The mark of the beast is on our head and hands, yet many are still looking for his appearing. I remember as a kid working in a grocery store where when scanners and computers were brought in many Christians saw this as a sign of the last days. The theory was that the new technology could easily be imprinted on people and many so called Bible prophets made millions selling their books and holding their seminars. You won't get the mark of the beast at the grocery store! You are more likely to get it watching television with your family or going to the movies as the harlot lures you in with her pleasures and her beauty. Have you noticed how television and the entertainment world are so forceful in projecting alternative lifestyles? At first we are offended, but in time it becomes normal. The church begins to set the standard for itself based on the world instead of the Word of God. We must be aware of the spiritual implications of these things. These attitudes and lifestyle choices become habitations for the enemy.

"For all the nations have drunk of the wine of the wrath of her fornication, the kings of the earth have committed fornication with her, and the merchants of the earth have become rich through the abundance of her luxury" (Revelation 18:3).

The governmental and business worlds are willing participates of the harlot's influence. Have you noticed how governments and businesses now seem to feel a compulsion to promote lifestyle choices contrary to the Word? The gay agenda is a good case in point. Why have so many big corporations been at the forefront of promoting alternative lifestyles? It certainly is not a business choice when it requires you to give benefits to people who are not legally married. You see the harlot of Babylon is also called mother. Unlike the church mother who seeks to bring children up for the pleasure of their father, this mother teaches her children to be harlots like her. Live for yourself; take advantage of your talents by selling them to the highest bidder. Life is not about service, but about pleasure. She teaches that we cannot have pleasure when we practice self-denial. The harlot doesn't promote responsibility but pleasure.

When Daniel and his companions came to Babylon they must have been overwhelmed. They were in the capitol of the great empire and saw the awesome accomplishments of the people. They were so amazing that the great Hanging Gardens of Babylon would be considered by the ancients as one of the "Seven Wonders of the World." Babylonian armies had destroyed the Holy City and even the temple. They had taken captive the treasuries and the crème of the crop as far as the people taken into the exile of the king's court. It must have been mesmerizing and awesome. But in the midst of the wonder they said, "We will live by the power of the Word. Even though our temple and city are destroyed, we will give our lives for the cause of God." Just like it was in those days so it is in our day. The power of the media, Wall Street money, and government seem so powerful and pervasive what can the church do to stem the tide? Many Christians have seemingly followed the, "can't win might as well join them" philosophy. Yet in the midst of this, God is also raising up a people who know their God and will do exploits in the anointing of the Holy Spirit.

When Daniel and his companions made the choice to follow God and His Word, at first, there was a time of testing. Will the Word be proven true? Afterward, opposition arose as jealousy, turning people against them. Shadrach, Meshach, and Abed-Nego were thrown into the burning furnace. This happened because they refused to allow Babylon to conform them to their ways. Against overwhelming odds, they determined not to fall to the system. When they were thrown into the furnace not only did God preserve them and keep them alive, but a great testimony came to the king and all his court. Daniel and his friends were promoted to great positions of authority and the name of God was glorified in Babylon.

It is exciting to me that many Christians are rising to the call to confront the harlot who is seducing the land. Christians are getting into the entertainment world, the business world, and government. It is not an easy task to do these things and be different. The world wants to conform us to her ways. They will try to make us feel we are inferior and out of touch. They will try to put a reproach upon us like the Egyptians did the children of Israel. They convinced them they were nobody until they were Egyptians. This reproach always made them feel the need to either go back to Egypt or to emulate them. When they built the golden calf in the wilderness they were looking to Egypt for their source of inspiration. But before they could enter the Promised Land the reproach had to be removed. They had to line up with the Word and go forth knowing it was God who would give the victory. It is time for victory. The day of the judgment of the harlot has come. We must come out of her and join the company of those who overcome.

How shall we overcome? We overcome by making ourselves ready for the Lamb. As the announcement of the judgment upon the harlot of Babylon is made, there also comes the announcement of the bride. When the bride has made herself ready by giving her heart fully to God, the Word of God will arise and serve the bride's enemies on a silver platter.

> *"Let us be glad and rejoice and give Him glory, for the marriage of the Lamb has come, and His wife has made herself ready." And to her it was granted to be arrayed in fine linen, clean and bright, for the fine linen is the righteous acts of the saints. Then he said to me, "Write: 'Blessed are those who are called to the marriage supper of the Lamb!'" And he said to*

me, "These are the true sayings of God." Then I saw an angel standing in the sun; and he cried with a loud voice, saying to all the birds that fly in the midst of heaven, "Come and gather together for the supper of the great God, that you may eat the flesh of kings, the flesh of captains, the flesh of mighty men, the flesh of horses and of those who sit on them, and the flesh of all people, free and slave, both small and great" (Revelation 19:7-9, 17-18).

Chapter Nine

THE DRAGON'S THRONE

In the book of 2 Corinthians Paul admonishes the church to forgive and to restore a fallen brother. He encouraged them to do this so satan would not have room to cause trouble and take advantage of them. He closes with, "for we are not ignorant of his devices." The purpose of this book is to help you understand the devil's devices so he cannot take advantage of you. The church has long held onto many myths and assumptions about the devil, and unless we let go of those myths and assumptions and begin to walk in understanding we will not be able to overcome the enemy as God desires. We know God will have a people who will be an overcoming people, but the question is will you be a part? If you are a Christian you will share in the victory, but the greater question is will you be an active son of God who will be part of the solution or will you be hiding in the back wondering what in the world is going on?

In Revelation chapter 13 we are told that the beast, who makes war on the people of God, will be given the power, throne, and authority of the dragon. Remember the dragon is identified in Revelation 12:9 as satan. This statement is very telling, but we must understand the meaning of satan's power, throne, and authority. As we have already learned, when Jesus Christ came to the earth He bound the strongman, satan, so we could make a spoil of his goods and repossess what he had taken. We must approach this verse with a full understanding of the Scriptures so we are not deceived by the enemy and intimidated by his person. A dragon is a dreadful looking creature, and the beast described in the book of Revelation leaves people saying, "who can make war with the beast?" From an outward appearance it would seem like no one can. However, we in the church, as the sons of God, cannot be intimidated by what we see, but we must be motivated by what we believe!

For many years I have watched the movie, *The Wizard of Oz*. I love the movie and the hopeful song the young girl sang, "Somewhere Over the Rainbow." The young girl and her companions faced many obstacles as they went in search of the Wizard of Oz whom they hoped would help them solve their predicament. When they came to the wizard's palace they saw a wild and awesome sight that scared them. As they stood in fear of the awesome sight the dog, Toto, went behind the scenes and found the wizard had no real power but had created a façade that held everyone under his spell. This is really what the picture of Revelation 13 is like. The beast is dreadful and terrible, yet the source of his power is the dragon and his throne, power, and authority. The problem with this scene is the same as with the Wizard of Oz. The strength of the beast is in a sense an illusion allowed by God for an appointed time. The time of his demise is when the church has made herself ready, the sons have cleaned up their act, and the time for the end has come. This end will involve the sons of God seeing their true identity and the power, authority, and throne that has been given to them!

> And they sang a new song, saying: "You are worthy to take the scroll, And to open its seals; For You were slain, And have redeemed us to God by Your blood Out of every tribe and tongue and people and nation, And have made us kings and priests to our God; And we shall reign on the earth" (Revelation 5:9-10).

When speaking of the beast the Scriptures tell us he is given authority over every tribe, tongue, and nation. To interpret this prophecy consistent with the biblical narrative, we must understand all authority originates with God. The devil's authority comes from the vacuum of mankind's disobedience to God. It is time for us to turn this ship around fully understanding what is in our hands and what God wants us to take from the enemy.

Many Christians in the past have interpreted this to mean there will one day be a world government that will fight against the church. This has left many prophecy teachers with the task of figuring out how this will happen. In my life I have witnessed many failed attempts to figure out how these nations will come together. The truth is the devil is the god of this world because all things outside the Kingdom of God have been given into his hand. There are many nations fully under his control that submit to his wishes, and they don't even know it. The Muslim nations that persecute the Christian church and foster world terrorism are fully under his control, yet they think they are the children of God doing God's work. Many of the European nations are bound to the enemies control through secular humanism and state socialism. These two systems of Islam and secularism seem in stark contrast to each other, yet the fruit of their works is the same. Both equally persecute and terrorize the Christian church whenever possible. It is interesting that the European continent, which was once the center of Christianity, takes a very strong antichristian stance, while at the same time will often feel obligated to placate the desires of the Muslim community. Do these two worlds need an alliance to fulfill the purposes of the devil?

Revelations 13 describes the beast as having some characteristics of a leopard, a bear, and a lion. The beast may not look like a single force, but in his operation he fulfills the devil's purpose. This is where the church needs to be more focused on the Word than the traditional concepts we have been guided by. From the very beginning the devil has always gone incognito. He always stays behind the scenes and is not immediately apparent.

Another mistaken notion people have is about the antichrist. As I already stated, it is important to understand there is not one antichrist but many. This isn't only a concept for the end times. As noted by the Apostle John, it was a real and present danger in his time. The Apostle Peter declared on the day of Pentecost that they

103

were in the last days as spoken of in the Scripture, but from a biblical point of view the last days are all the days from the day of Jesus' resurrection to the day of His appearing.

The idea that the devil will finally appear in the form of a world leader is also another tradition that will cause us to miss what God is doing and cause us to live in fear and apprehension concerning these latter days of time. The devil has always used people, but to actually manifest himself in a person does not have biblical precedent. Sometimes evil is personified through individuals. When you look over the last century there is no question evil manifested itself through the likes of Adolf Hitler, Motze Tung, and Joseph Stalin. Without question, the systems that gave rise to these people were instigated through the devil's influence. But if we focus on a person, we will miss what the enemy is all about for he goes throughout the whole earth seeking whom he may devour.

The Bible in Deuteronomy 32:8 tells us that God sets the borders of the nations. When sending out the disciples they were instructed to disciple the "nations." There is no biblical basis to believe the day will come when one person will control the nations. In speaking of the latter days the Bible declares "all nations" shall flow to the house of God. Although as Christians we are called out of our heritage into the Kingdom of God, it is very appropriate to recognize governments as agents of God that He has established for our good.

> *Let every soul be subject to the governing authorities. For there is no authority except from God, and the authorities that exist are appointed by God. Therefore whoever resists the authority resists the ordinance of God, and those who resist will bring judgment on themselves. For rulers are not a terror to good works, but to evil. Do you want to be unafraid of the authority? Do what is good, and you will have praise from the same. For he is God's minister to you for good. But if you do evil, be afraid; for he does not bear the sword in vain; for he is God's minister, an avenger to execute wrath on him who practices evil* (Romans 13:1-4).

We witnessed at the close of the cold war the re-emergence of many nations. Today there are more nations than we have seen in a long time. Is this a sign we are not in the last days, or is it a sign that God is once again establishing the nations so His Word can come to pass in this day? We should not be fighting a battle to save the world but the individual nations. The devil knows this more than anybody. God has ordained that each nation have their own individual call and purpose. As Christians we need strategies for the nations of the earth so each nation can fulfill the purpose God has called them to.

Just as we must recognize the purpose for the nations, we must also see how the devil uses this concept for his purpose. Revelation 13:7 talks about tribes, tongues, and nations. It is interesting that in every nation there are tribes or small distinct groups, languages or ethnic differences, as well as national identities. God is a God who instigates diversity. From the beginning when God created Eve, who was taken out of man, God has put things in other people we need. As with Adam and Eve each is given different roles but equal status. The Bible tells us God made man and woman in His image and likeness. The hierarchy of dominion of one over the other was a result of the fall. This hierarchy is necessary when we go outside the bounds of God's covenant. Notice the example of the children of Israel in the Old Testament. God created a people or nation for Himself. In that nation there were twelve tribes each one having a specific characteristic and call. When Jacob blessed his sons in Genesis 49 he identified the major characteristics of each son and told of the impact their genetics had on them and would have on their seed in the last days. Each tribe of the earth has genetic influences one needs to recognize and also tame for the glory of God.

The way the devil takes advantage of these differences is through the same methods he uses on the individual. In the Garden of Eden the devil persuaded Eve to believe that the way to true happiness was taking control of her life. Mankind was told not to depend on God or trust Him, but that the key was to gain knowledge and control. Motivated by the appeal of pride and fleshly satisfaction the enemy gained his foothold and, of course, the rest is history.

This is also the pattern by which he controls nations. The devil encourages nations and tribes to seek to exalt themselves and take control. People easily fall prey to the idea that they are better or more deserving than others. The end of this is a usurping of control over others so you can take advantage of them.

The classic example of this was in the 1930's when Hitler convinced the Germans they were a superior race and should be in control of the world. The people succumbed to this lie because of the harsh economic times and a desire to see their physical needs met. Hitler offered them the world. The horrors of this sin were fully manifested through the mass murders of other races and people, especially those of Jewish descent who lost around six million people. Yet the vastness of the suffering was not limited to one group. Sin and rebellion will always lead to death. The only winner in that effort was the devil.

As World War II came to a close the devil had already had his next victims on deck. Just like in Revelation 13 where one beast goes another is sure to follow. The Russian people, also in response to economic hardship, had turned to communism for their salvation. Although communism was an atheistic movement, the people were more concerned about their stomachs than their souls. An interesting observation of this time is that communism, in the end, was not really the force behind the Soviet Empire. Although communism and world revolution was the theme, the truth is the Russians were simply using their philosophy as a cover for the ethnic motivations the Russian people had for centuries. This cause only gave them a noble theme to continue to be the empire builders they had been throughout history. It is important to again note that the devil is good at inventing noble causes that will in the end find their strength in more base human intentions. The Soviet Empire was simply a state government that replaced one ruling elite with another. The privileged class were now the party leaders rather than the former aristocrats, but the actual country did not change much. This obviously became clear when the Soviet Empire fell and the new government took power. Alas, Russia was still Russia with a different form of government again. This is why understanding our culture and history are vital to our seeing satan's devices. If we have a weakness the enemy will surely seize it as an opportunity for his purpose to be fulfilled.

As the devil has national strategies, so it is important for the church to have national strategies as well. God wants us to disciple nations by turning them to Christ, breaking the strongholds of the enemy, and then helping them fulfill their own destiny. I find it interesting how God will give people burdens for certain nations. Sometimes it is a burden of their own choosing, and other times it is a burden that seems to come out of nowhere. God has a heart for the nations and He wants us to have one too. I have found that human motivations are normally good; it is just where we take them that turn something good into something bad.

Although we should love nations, we must be careful of nationalism. This is what comes from the human need to be superior and control others. Nationalism has been the root of many wars and divisions in the earth. Nationalism generally is when we associate one ethnic group with a territory and have a perception based on the primary importance of that group. This can result in ethnic cleansing as witnessed in Germany in World War II and in Yugoslavia after the fall of the iron curtain. Each state that evolved from the dissolved Yugoslavia sought to preserve a homeland for their own ethnic group. This often leads to a desire for a homogenous national culture leading to persecution of people who are different.

I am a resident of the United States of America, and although we are a so-called, melting pot of nations, many times the predominant groups have tried to maintain the status quo by holding others down. The most glaring example was the marginalization of the African American community even after they were liberated by the civil war. Nationalism can be a stronghold of the devil to incite many evils. Most nations and cultures have been guilty of giving in to this trap at one time or another.

It is interesting how, even in the Christian church itself, we have often tried to maintain a homogenous community. This was the condition Jesus Christ came to when He came to the children of Israel. Their desire for a homogenous community had led to excluding many people from God. Jesus Christ showed us how to deal with this in the story of the woman at the well. She was a Samaritan woman with a colorful past, having five husbands and living with someone who was not her husband, when she met Jesus. Much to the amazement of the woman and others, Jesus broke through every barrier to bring her to the Kingdom. Jesus didn't turn her into a Jew, but He did turn her to God. She turned her city to God after that. When we turn people to God through the proclamation of the gospel we are giving the devil a deadly punch. Like Jesus Christ before us, let us lay aside anything that separates us from God and let's help others do the same. In the end we will see two harvests. There will be the harvest of the righteous and the harvest of the wicked. I know what harvest I want to be in. I also want to be a participant in this great day of God's visitation on the nations.

Chapter Ten

THE ANGEL OF LIGHT

It is very important that we understand the devil's personification, or in other words, how he represents himself. From the beginning, in the Garden of Eden, he has presented himself as someone who is on our side. This is why I believe we need to be careful not to think of the devil as an actual serpent or dragon. Believing this persona is the root cause of our weakness, which allows us to be deceived by him. What I am about to say will offend many and put you on guard, but please carefully consider something very important in the battle against evil. When the devil comes he comes as an angel of light not as a messenger of darkness. In our popular culture and in religious themes throughout history, satan and the devil have been portrayed as dark figures rather than a figure of light. This personification in the end makes us think his deceptions are always easy to see and avoid. The opposite is true. One of the devil's greatest tricks is to play on our fear of the dark side of his person while he comes to us as a person of light and gains his foothold.

Halloween is considered a dreadful holiday for many Christians because of the association with the devil and the power of darkness. The devil and his demons are portrayed as creatures of evil with the devil often wearing a red suit and carrying a pitchfork. Many churches refrain from Halloween celebrations because of the association with the darkness. The problem with Halloween celebrations is actually just the opposite of what people think. This principle is demonstrated by the way many churches respond to the problem. In response to the darkness of Halloween, rather than have Halloween parties they have harvest parties so people will dress in more appropriate disguises. The unfortunate thing is that these harvest parties demonstrate how we often fall prey to the devil's devices and we don't even realize it. You see when the devil comes to church he always knows he has to dress like a saint or Christian if he is going to have any influence. When the devil comes to your world he will always dress in a friendly and approachable form. He wants to fit in, not stand out. He wants to be one of us not someone on the outside. A good object lesson would be to have a traditional "worldly" celebration with the customary demons and devils then announce who the real devil is. This devil should be dressed as an angel, deacon, cheerleader, sports figure, or better yet, a little old lady. If the devil is at work in your church that is what he will look like! The traditional personas were created to make people learn the fear of the world of darkness, but in the end they have lulled us to sleep giving us a false impression of who the devil really is!

In the context of calling satan the angel of light, the Apostle Paul is talking about false apostles and deceitful workers who transform themselves into the messengers of Christ. It is so important that we are a people on guard and aware of the devil's devices but also to those of his messengers. The Apostle Paul spoke of a "messenger of satan" who was sent to buffet him. This word in the original context is from the same word we get angel. Paul's thorn in the flesh was obviously a person he wanted out of his life. When you read the letters of the apostle you will see he had much opposition within the churches he fathered and in which he was the overseer. Often times he had to write and deal with the people in the midst of the churches who were resisting his authority even though he was the father over them. I am sure many of these same people were not aware who they were working for. Not only does the devil come as a messenger of light, he is an expert in the Word of God. The devil loves "noble" causes because he can get people to rally around the light of his cause, and people will resist God thinking they are doing God a favor. The Apostle Paul himself was at one point caught up in this deception.

"Indeed, I myself thought I must do many things contrary to the name of Jesus of Nazareth. This I also did in Jerusalem, and many of the saints I shut up in prison, having received authority from the chief priests; and when they were put to death, I cast my vote against them" (Acts 26:9-10).

One of the things I have noticed about people in the 31 years I have been a pastor is that people love to take sides. Taking sides in a conflict gives people a sense of closeness to other people, which satisfies our natural affiliation needs. When we are in the midst of a problem it is also natural for us to want to have people on our side. This affirmation encourages us in our choices. With these two human needs working together, it makes it very common for conflicts to arise and bring division to the body of Christ and resistance to the move of God. The devil and his messengers are always standing by waiting to take advantage of these opportunities. These conflicts should be easy to identify as the works of the flesh mentioned in Galatians chapter 5.

Now the works of the flesh are evident, . . . idolatry, sorcery, hatred, contentions, jealousies, outbursts of wrath, selfish ambitions, dissensions, heresies, . . . and the like; of which I tell you beforehand, just as I also told you in time past, that those who practice such things will not inherit the kingdom of God (Galatians 5:19, 20, 21).

Unfortunately, because we tie our actions to noble causes we easily become the prey of the devil. I grew up in a small church that wanted to become more evangelistic and grow. In the end, the noble efforts were often stymied by strife and division motivated by personal ambitions. The church remained for many years as a testimony of frustrated efforts for the Kingdom of God. If you really want to do something for the Lord you must understand there is only one side and that is God's side. Joshua, the leader chosen to take the children of Israel into the Promised Land, had to understand this principle before he could lead the children of Israel into the land. One day as he was standing next to Jericho, the first city they had to defeat, Joshua came face to face with someone whose sword was drawn opposite him.

> *And it came to pass, when Joshua was by Jericho, that he lifted his eyes and looked, and behold, a Man stood opposite him with His sword drawn in His hand. And Joshua went to Him and said to Him, "Are You for us or for our adversaries?" So He said, "No, but as Commander of the army of the LORD I have now come." And Joshua fell on his face to the earth and worshiped, and said to Him, "What does my Lord say to His servant?"* (Joshua 5:13-14).

Joshua's immediate response to his situation was to try and find out whose side the person was on. Isn't this such a typical response when we face confrontations in life? The announcement is clear there is only one side, God's. This message came from none other than God Himself so Joshua fell down and worshipped Him. Often when people are taking sides they are deceived by believing they are on God's side. The first question is, what is the fruit or result of the action taken. Secondly, can we discern self-centered motivations? When Jesus, the New Testament Joshua, was getting ready to take His promised land He began to prepare His disciples by letting them know what was to come. Peter wanted to get on "His" side, so to speak, by letting Him know he would be there to defend Him. Peter actually rebuked the Lord and said, "This shall not happen to you." I'll protect you and fight for you was basically Peter's claim. Unfortunately, Peter was becoming the enemy of Jesus Christ because the truth of the situation was Jesus needed to suffer and die to fulfill the Father's purpose for Him. This is why it may have seemed harsh, but look at what Jesus had to say:

> *But He turned and said to Peter, "Get behind Me , Satan! You are an offense to Me, for you are not mindful of the things of God, but the things of men"* (Matthew 16:23).

112

Jesus went on to tell the greater truth:

Then Jesus said to His disciples, "If anyone desires to come after Me, let him deny himself, and take up his cross, and follow Me. For whoever desires to save his life will lose it, but whoever loses his life for My sake will find it (Matthew 16:24-25).

When God is on your side you don't need anyone else to win the battle. You do need to guard your heart so that the issue is not your needs and desires but God's. Jesus gave us this example by what He said and by what He did. Satan gains his foothold when people allow a situation to be about them. Again, if the devil can get us into the center he has already won the war. This is why Jesus Christ is the way, the truth, and the life. Life comes by giving God His way and letting His word be the truth. When we take up the Word as our sword it often becomes a tool for self-centered motivations. When we allow the Word to stand as truth it will stand alone and ultimately bring the victory. If you believe in the truth you know that in the end truth will prevail.

The Apostle John warned about the antichrist in 1 John 2:18:

Little children, it is the last hour; and as you have heard that the Antichrist is coming, even now many antichrists have come, by which we know that it is the last hour. They went out from us, but they were not of us; for if they had been of us, they would have continued with us; but they went out that they might be made manifest, that none of them were of us (1 John 2:18-19).

Even today many people fear the antichrist, and yet, the apostle affirms there are many antichrists not one. The word antichrist comes from two words, to stand opposite and Christ. The word Christ here would not only be Jesus Himself but also His body, the church, the fullness of Him who fills all as the Scriptures declare. Note the antichrists are those who were once with us. The antichrist does not come from the world but from the church. They stand against Christ's anointed. In this position they certainly become satan's messengers as they seek to destroy the church by standing in opposition to the truth. They will begin their rebellion with a side of the truth. Remember the truth will always have more than one side. If two people are in an argument the reason for the conflict is most likely both have a side of the truth. Rather than embracing truth in its entirely they will seek to be right and draw others to their side. This is why unbiased council is so important, because it can bring opposing sides together. The truth is not that hard to find. When we have the Holy Spirit we have the Spirit of Truth, and if we will honestly reflect on the truth it will manifest itself.

> *But you have an anointing from the Holy One, and you know all things. I have not written to you because you do not know the truth, but because you know it, and that no lie is of the truth. These things I have written to you concerning those who try to deceive you. But the anointing which you have received from Him abides in you, and you do not need that anyone teach you; but as the same anointing teaches you concerning all things, and is true, and is not a lie, and just as it has taught you, you will abide in Him (1 John 2:20-21, 26-27).*

It is during conflicts, especially in the church, that satan's influence is revealed. Speaking again of a topic most people tend to apply only to the last days, the Apostle Paul addresses this issue with the church of Thessalonica. They were in confusion believing perhaps the Lord had already come and they had missed it. The apostle begins to share principles that certainly apply to the last day when satan and his works will be utterly destroyed, but they are also principles we need to understand in our on going conflict to finish off the work Jesus started when He came to earth to bind the strongman. In order for the devil and his works to be destroyed, they must first be revealed. This process begins with a falling away.

114

Let no one deceive you by any means; for that Day will not come unless the falling away comes first, and the man of sin is revealed, the son of perdition . . . (2 Thessalonians 2:3).

The words "falling away" here means to leave the truth. It speaks of separation. The NIV calls it the rebellion. This can be seen in society as a whole, who rebel against the truth of the Word. It can also be seen in a church split or family breakup. The man of sin and his messengers would rather destroy and cause division and loss than to accept something other than their personal ambition being fulfilled. These underlying ambitions always exist, but God holds them in check till He is ready to reveal the truth and bring those in opposition under judgment.

And now you know what is restraining, that he may be revealed in his own time. For the mystery of lawlessness is already at work; only He who now restrains will do so until He is taken out of the way. And then the lawless one will be revealed, whom the Lord will consume with the breath of His mouth and destroy with the brightness of His coming (2 Thessalonians 2:6-8).

The pattern is the same. God allows the enemy to have a voice so those who choose to may follow his deceptions. Remember, we don't have to believe the lies of the devil. God's spirit will let us know the truth if we want to see it. Unfortunately, the devil has power because we give him room.

The coming of the lawless one is according to the working of Satan, with all power, signs, and lying wonders, and with all unrighteous deception among those who perish, because they did not receive the love of the truth, that they might be saved. And for this reason God will send them strong delusion, that they should believe the lie, that they all may be condemned who did not believe the truth but had pleasure in unrighteousness (2 Thessalonians 2:9-12).

115

If we want to stand strong in the last days we can practice for that day on a regular basis. The lawless one is always at work, and we need to learn of his devises and resist him. In this case we resist him by loving the truth.

Why does the devil spend so much time in church? The church is the center and focus of all God has for the earth. He has the world, but he is mad and makes war with the woman and her seed. It is an attempt to stop our participation in the eternal purposes of God.

> *. . . to the intent that now the manifold wisdom of God might be made known by the church to the principalities and powers in the heavenly places, according to the eternal purpose which He accomplished in Christ Jesus our Lord . . .* (Ephesians 3:10-11)

All the eyes of the heavenly realm are looking for the revelation of God's divine wisdom through the church. This is why the devil is here at work trying to stop us from fulfilling our part of the divine plan. If the devil can get you out of church he has effectively taken you out of the will and purpose of God. The church and the behavior of the church is the ground of everything God is doing.

> *. . . but if I am delayed, I write so that you may know how you ought to conduct yourself in the house of God, which is the church of the living God, the pillar and ground of the truth* (1 Timothy 3:15).

Yet, we must understand God is not the only one planting seeds in the earth. Jesus spoke about this in the parable of the wheat and the tares.

> *Another parable He put forth to them, saying: "The kingdom of heaven is like a man who sowed good seed in his field; but while men slept, his enemy came and sowed tares among the wheat and went his way. But when the grain had sprouted and produced a crop, then the tares also appeared. So the ser-*

vants of the owner came and said to him, 'Sir, did you not sow good seed in your field? How then does it have tares?' He said to them, 'An enemy has done this.' The servants said to him, 'Do you want us then to go and gather them up?' But he said, 'No, lest while you gather up the tares you also uproot the wheat with them. Let both grow together until the harvest, and at the time of harvest I will say to the reapers, "First gather together the tares and bind them in bundles to burn them, but gather the wheat into my barn" (Matthew 13:24-30).

This is a very important concept in the Kingdom of God. There are bad seeds in the church, but remember our job is not to weed them out. We are not suppose to decide who is good or bad, but we are responsible to judge good and bad behavior and make every effort to be a part of the work of God. In the end God will always judge the unrighteous acts of men, but as I have already stated it will first serve a purpose in the divine economy. The word heresy in the Bible, in the original context, does not mean to have a false doctrine. The word actually means to be over opinionated. You take the Word of God or some noble cause and use it to bring division. What good could heresy have in the church? Paul tells us:

For there must be also heresies among you, that they which are approved may be made manifest among you (1 Corinthians 11:19 KJV).

We all need to ask ourselves the question. What are we manifesting in our life? Just as we understand as Christians that we are the children of God, it is important to note the devil has children too! When the Jewish people stood in opposition to Jesus Christ resisting the truth, He didn't just call them bad children. He told them they were of their father, the devil.

You do the deeds of your father. "Then they said to Him, 'We were not born of fornication; we have one Father—God.'" Jesus said to them, "If God were your Father, you would love

Me, for I proceeded forth and came from God; nor have I come of Myself, but He sent Me. Why do you not understand My speech? Because you are not able to listen to My word. You are of your father the devil, and the desires of your father you want to do. He was a murderer from the beginning, and does not stand in the truth, because there is no truth in him. When he speaks a lie, he speaks from his own resources, for he is a liar and the father of it (John 8:41-44).

The Apostle John heard these words as he recorded them in his gospel and fully affirmed them in his epistle. He understood our parentage is not who we claim but what is manifested in our life.

He who sins is of the devil, for the devil has sinned from the beginning. For this purpose the Son of God was manifested, that He might destroy the works of the devil. In this the children of God and the children of the devil are manifest. Whoever does not practice righteousness is not of God, nor is he who does not love his brother (1 John 3:8, 10).

Jesus Christ is our example. When He was manifested He literally came to destroy the works of the devil. Now we, the seed of the woman, are under the assault of the evil one, but it is written, "We will overcome!" The victory is ours. We just need to begin to walk in the fullness of the victory Christ has purchased for us!

Chapter Eleven

ARISE AND SHINE

In Conclusion

Isaiah the prophet declares:

Arise, shine; For your light has come! And the glory of the LORD is risen upon you. For behold, the darkness shall cover the earth, And deep darkness the people; But the LORD will arise over you, And His glory will be seen upon you. he Gentiles shall come to your light And kings to the brightness of your rising (Isaiah 60:1-3).

When contemplating our call from God we need to understand the principles laid out in these verses. The people of God must be proactive in our approach to life. In the beginning God created man in His image and likeness and called us to be fruitful, multiply, and fill up the earth. We are also given a mandate of dominion. It is through our godlikeness that we are to move forward and take our place in the purposes of God. This is why we must see the light "has come" and we must move forward in the light and power of the Word of God. This will cause the world to see the work of God and be drawn to the testimony of His power and glory in the church.

Concerning the darkness we should consider as a matter of fact that the "darkness will cover the earth and deep darkness the people." The words deep darkness in the original translation speak of the influence of the darkness upon the people's emotional state.

In the end dark behavior produces dark emotions. Rather then being darkness conscious as we have so often been in the past we, the church, need to see how this works in the plan and purpose of God. The darkness in the midst of His people provides the contrast to draw people to the glory of God and this darkness inflicts a burden on them that will ultimately give them the incentive to turn to God in their adversity.

We are living in the latter days of history when we will see the fulfillment of all the things God has spoken through the mouth of the prophets. Jesus will not come nor will the end of all things until all God has purposed has come to pass.

> *Repent therefore and be converted, that your sins may be blotted out, so that times of refreshing may come from the presence of the Lord, and that He may send Jesus Christ, who was preached to you before, whom heaven must receive until the times of restoration of all things, which God has spoken by the mouth of all His holy prophets since the world began* (Acts 3:19-21).

It is vitally important we, the church, understand the purposes of God and how we are to fit into that purpose. What God has purposed will come to pass.

> *Then Job answered the LORD and said: "I know that You can do everything, And that no purpose of Yours can be withheld from You"* (Job 42:1-2).

God has a purpose for us and I am fully convinced because it is His purpose it will certainly come to pass. It is also vitally important that we understand all things are factored into His plan. It is best for us to always be looking for the God given purpose of things rather than have a mindset that leads us to think something is outside the plans and purposes of God. When we understand that all things exist as part of the plan and purpose of God we approach our understanding of darkness from this perspective. Our confidence is that in the end everything will be for the glory of God!

The Word of God declares the progressive enlightenment we will see as the purposes of God unfold in the earth.

And so we have the prophetic word confirmed, which you do well to heed as a light that shines in a dark place, until the day dawns and the morning star rises in your hearts . . . (2 Peter 1:19).

As we move forward in the plans and purposes of God in this day we must understand the importance of the increasing light. We must allow ourselves to walk in this increasing light and also receive the fresh perspective of the Word of God that will need to come to us to fully walk in the blessing of this time. It will certainly become more clear as the glory of God becomes evident to us that God's sovereignty must be unquestioned and that in the end His wisdom will not only be manifest to us but to all of creation.

. . . and to make all see what is the fellowship of the mystery, which from the beginning of the ages has been hidden in God who created all things through Jesus Christ; to the intent that now the manifold wisdom of God might be made known by the church to the principalities and powers in the heavenly places, according to the eternal purpose which He accomplished in Christ Jesus our Lord . . . (Ephesians 3:9-11).

The message of the last book of the Bible is the message of the overcomer. He who overcomes will inherit all things. We cannot be an overcomer without understanding the purposes of God and the enemy we face in taking possession of the promises of God. We must be careful not to underestimate the influence of the devil, but we must also be very careful not to overstate his power. We must not let people continue to view evil from the perspective of man-made traditions and superstition. Jesus told the people of His day they were making the Word of God void by their traditions. I think this is amazing that the Word can be so powerful yet in our lives we can negate this power simply because our mindsets are built on tradition and past religious experiences. This is the dawning of a new day.

121

Will you be open and let God give you the light of His Word so you can walk in the victory God has for your life?

> *O house of Jacob, come and let us walk In the light of the LORD* (Isaiah 2:5).

I have explained the importance of our proper relationship to darkness in this book. We understand darkness is not just the absence of light but that it also becomes the binding force of the things outside the will and purpose of God. This understanding maintains the clear witness of the difference between light and darkness and also demonstrates the foolishness of walking outside the will and the purpose of God. The places of darkness are positioned awaiting the shining of the light of God. This light in the end will fully dispel darkness and bring the end of all things standing in opposition to the will and purpose of God. In order for this to be manifested the important message to the church is for us to understand our need to fully walk in the light and to ultimately be the sons of light in our world.

> *Then Jesus said to them, "A little while longer the light is with you. Walk while you have the light, lest darkness overtake you; he who walks in darkness does not know where he is going. While you have the light, believe in the light, that you may become sons of light"* (John 12:35-36).

For too long the church has tried to fight the darkness without true long-term results. We need to shine the light. How easily Adam and Eve could have defeated the devil in the garden. All they had to do was obey God and darkness would have been held in place. It is interesting to me as I have observed the charismatic and Pentecostal movements spending so much time trying to figure out how to defeat the devil and simple obedience is overlooked. In our efforts to defeat the devil we have made a lot of noise while the enemy has been invading the church. Simple obedience to the Word of God is being ignored, as the church has become more a place of human interest rather than the place to pursue the Kingdom of

God. The Scripture tells us when we seek first the Kingdom of God and His righteousness all the things of life will be added to us. Our struggle according to the Words of Jesus Christ is to "press into the Kingdom."

> *"The law and the prophets were until John. Since that time the kingdom of God has been preached, and everyone is pressing into it. And it is easier for heaven and earth to pass away than for one tittle of the law to fail"* (Luke 16:16-17).

When contemplating the battle of the Christian experience we should see it as the battle to press into the Kingdom of God. Our militant attitude must be to be vigilant as a soldier going after the kingdom not going after the devil.

> *And from the days of John the Baptist until now the kingdom of heaven suffers violence, and the violent take it by force* (Matthew 11:12).

It is the Kingdom of God we are called to take not the kingdom or realm of the enemy. This is the picture given in the beginning in the Garden of Eden. God placed man in the garden to tend and keep it. When man was disobedient he was kicked out of the garden. Now we are pressing to get back into the place God has for us. The devil is given a place by the absence of our stewardship not by his ability to steal or take something from us. One of the most misquoted scriptures of the Bible is found in John chapter 10:

> *All who ever came before Me are thieves and robbers, but the sheep did not hear them. I am the door. If anyone enters by Me, he will be saved, and will go in and out and find pasture. The thief does not come except to steal, and to kill, and to destroy. I have come that they may have life, and that they may have it more abundantly* (John 10:8-10).

These Scriptures are often quoted to describe the work of the devil when they are actually talking about false prophets, teachers, and pastors. The attitudes and motivations of these false leaders can certainly fall prey to the devil's devices but are actually more influenced by the human rather than the demonic.

The Kingdom of God is the place where God's will is fully followed and this includes our heart motivations. We must not only seek His will but also His righteousness, which involves following God not just from the letter of the Word but also from the Spirit. This is where the temptations of an enemy can be helpful to the plan of God because in the temptation we are able to face not only our actions but our motivations! This is why the enemy not only tests our obedience but reveals our hearts. When our heart is manifested to us and it reveals a need for change then we have the mercy and grace of God available to us to allow us access to His presence and also His power to change. But the Word of God clearly states that those who want to believe a lie and hold to unrighteousness will fall prey to their desires and will be consumed by the darkness.

> *The coming of the lawless one is according to the working of Satan, with all power, signs, and lying wonders, and with all unrighteous deception among those who perish, because they did not receive the love of the truth, that they might be saved. And for this reason God will send them strong delusion, that they should believe the lie, that they all may be condemned who did not believe the truth but had pleasure in unrighteousness* (2 Thessalonians 2:9-12).

We are living in the days when satan's seat or authority will not only be revealed but will be dispelled by the brightness of our rising. The Lord will arise through us before He descends for the final end of this age. We are living in the time when we must fully manifest the power and glory for which Jesus Christ Himself died. He came to destroy the works of the devil. We will crush satan under our feet not through great prayers of faith but by submitting ourselves to the righteousness of God.

Little children, let no one deceive you. He who practices right-eousness is righteous, just as He is righteous. He who sins is of the devil, for the devil has sinned from the beginning. For this purpose the Son of God was manifested, that He might destroy the works of the devil (1 John 3:7-8).

One aspect of the need for darkness is so the children of God can be manifested or revealed. Darkness also reveals the sons of the devil. This is the time of the manifestation. What will your life manifest?

Other Books by Loren Covarrubias

ABOUT FATHER'S HOUSE

A book written to help the author's local church, Mt. Zion, see how God as a Father, cares for his people and has a plan for them.

DISCOVERING FAVOR WITH GOD

This book offers simple keys to experiencing God's love for you.